DORDT INFOR
3 6520
D0328918

THE SECRET OF CHRISTIAN FAMILY LIVING

THE SECRET OF CHRISTIAN FAMILY LIVING

by
Ralph Heynen

DORDT COLLEGE
LIBRARY
Sioux Center, Iowa

BAKER BOOK HOUSE
Grand Rapids, Michigan

22787

Library of Congress Catalog Card Number: 65-16377

First printing, March 1965
Second printing, May 1966

Copyright, 1965, by
Baker Book House Company

PRINTED IN THE UNITED STATES OF AMERICA

Gratefully dedicated to the memory of
my parents,
The Rev. and Mrs. Henry J. Heynen,
who laid firm foundations for mental
and spiritual health in their home;
and to
The Rev. and Mrs. William P. Van Wyk,
who welcomed me as a son into a
family which warmly radiated the influence
of constructive Christian living.

Preface

For more than two decades my parish has been a hospital, and my parishioners were men, women and children who were sick. Some were more seriously ill than others, but each one was struggling with some emotional, mental or spiritual problem. During these years many people, from every walk of life, came to this "city of the sick" and found help and healing and solace.

Counseling with those who face the crisis experiences of life is a challenging and rewarding ministry. Chaplains have the privilege of entering intimately into the lives of people, to establish relationships that can be healthy and wholesome.

In every person with emotional and mental conflicts the home and family relationships also play their role. In some it is involved in the immediate cause of the breakdown. In others the earliest impressions made upon the person were not wholesome. Others failed to learn to face up to the frustrations of life with the needed strength and courage.

The family is our number-one cause of emotional disease. It can also be the number-one factor in promoting emotional and mental health. The home lays down the basic fundamentals upon which a personality must be built. It has well been stated that "the home is the university of the emotions."

It is then not surprising to observe that in an age when the family and the home are being weakened, there should be an increase in admissions into mental hospitals. Psychiatrists, psychologists, social workers, family and pastoral counselors all carry a large number of clients, and many of these have problems in their family life.

This would possibly account for the fact that there are many younger people who are enrolled in mental institutions. Most hospitals are treating a goodly number of adolescents with problems of adjustment. Many young fathers and mothers also need the care and treatment of hospitals today due to problems of family adjustment in this tense generation.

It is the purpose of this volume to show the relationship between mental health and family living. Our Christian view of mental and emotional health speaks to the family as a unit, and to the family in its functions in the social and cultural structure.

The chapters of this book first appeared as articles in *The Banner,* a weekly church periodical, published by the Christian Reformed Publishing House. It is with the kind permission of the Board of Publication and the encouragement of the editor, the Rev. John Vander Ploeg, that some of these articles are presented in this form.

The generous reception given to a previous volume, *The Art of Christian Living* (Baker, 1963) has been most gratifying and inspiring. This volume is sent forth with the prayer that it will help to promote greater interest in the practice of Christian mental health in our homes.

RALPH HEYNEN

Contents

THE FAMILY AS A UNIT

PARENTS AND THEIR CHILDREN

TEEN-AGERS IN THE HOME

THE FAMILY AS A UNIT

Marriage, then, is a Divine ordinance
intended to be a source of happiness to man,
an institution of the highest significance to the human race,
and a symbol of the union of Christ and His Church.
We may, therefore, as Christians look with confidence
for grace in the discharge of our mutual responsibilities
and for guidance in our common perplexities and trials.

From a Marriage Form

1. Building a Christian Marriage

Today one out of every four marriages in the United States ends in divorce. Without a doubt, this increase in marital difficulties has not left the church unscarred. Difficulties in family life seem to be on the increase. You can be sure, if one marriage in four climaxes in divorce, that there is much strife and conflict in many homes, even though it does not lead to such tragic results.

This is not a pretty picture, for it indicates that one of the greatest bulwarks of the Christian life is being attacked. It is hard to describe what such conditions can do to the sensitive and impressionable emotions of children as the victims of these difficulties.

WHAT IS A CHRISTIAN MARRIAGE?

A good criterion of a successful marriage is that it can contribute to the personalities of the marriage partners and can prove to be a suitable place for children to be reared.

J. K. Morris in a book, *Pre-Marital Counseling,* gives the following definition of a Christian marriage: "A Christian marriage is one involving a Christian man and woman, each dedicated to his understanding of God's purpose for himself and his spouse, and their children, to achieve the measure of the fulness of the stature in Christ." He goes on, "In a marriage that is truly Christian both the husband and the wife will respect the developing personality of the other, aid its enhancement, strengthen it where it is weak and encourage it in its goodness."

One of the great requirements for a successful marriage is that the two parties complement each other in the physical, mental, emotional and spiritual factors of life. Such a view stresses the positive purpose of marriage as being the "mutual enrichment of the lives of those entering this state." This puts it in a different light from that which is so common in American life where, for many, marriage is based on physical attraction and the recitation of certain prescribed vows.

MARRIAGE IS AN ACHIEVEMENT

A Christian marriage does not just happen. It is a matter that requires consecrated effort. It is something that cannot just be taken for granted.

It requires of us the very highest form of acceptance and adjustment. For, here is one of the very closest interpersonal relationships of life. It stands to reason that certain adjustments are needed on the part of both husband and wife. In wedded life there are two people, from different homes and different family backgrounds, often with different standards of living and conduct, and these two lives are blended together into one.

Some people do not adjust very well to others, and to changes in life. This is often one of the basic causes of difficulties between husband and wife. Some people just want to have everything go their own way, and such people make poor materials for the cooperative venture of setting up a home.

ITS BASIC INGREDIENT – LOVE

Much is made today of a romantic type of love, the kind of love that is portrayed in modern novels, poems and songs. This is often the love that would be manifested in courtship, rather than in marriage. But marriage is not just a continued courtship nor a constant honeymoon.

The love in marriage is a more mature love; it is not just the love of the heart. It also requires an act of the will. The Bible speaks of loving with "heart and soul and mind and strength." The wedding form implies this when the bridal couple is asked to promise to love "as long as you both shall live." This is a love that exercises all the qualities of the soul.

Sometimes one of the marriage partners will say, "Well, I just don't love him any more." That is part of the idea of falling in love, or falling out of love again. This is the romantic type of love, and it is not a sufficient basis for a good marriage. It requires also an act of the will to truly love.

Here lies the strength of a Christian marriage. For, the love of a Christian bridal couple is one that is hallowed by a love for God. This views marriage then not only on a horizontal plane, but also on a vertical one.

A PERFECT MARRIAGE?

There has never yet been a perfect marriage; it cannot be so, because there has never been a perfect husband or a perfect wife. There may be ideal marriages, which seem to rise above the average. But even there, there are difficulties and differences that arise. They are bound to occur.

Character faults soon become evident in married life, even though they may not be evident to those who stand outside the home circle. But it is also true that our own weaknesses become evident. Here the Christian marriage has a tower of strength in the attitude that grows from the spirit of forgiveness.

We must learn to accept our mate in wedded life for what he or she is, not just what we would like to have them be. But with this attitude, neither the husband nor his wife need be afraid to admit that he has failings and sins, for there is always the feeling that we are willing to forgive in the same way that we seek forgiveness from our Father in heaven.

This leads to true Christian acceptance of each other. This is the pathway of true love, and a fitting foundation for a Christian marriage.

2. Adjustments in Marriage

Many articles appear in magazines on how to get along in marriage. One of these was entitled "How to Be Happy Even Though Married." Another magazine made things easy by presenting "Ten Rules for Getting Along with Your Wife," and in the next issue "Ten Rules for Getting Along with Your Husband." I enjoyed the one that appeared in a popular journal about a year ago entitled "But I Love to Quarrel with My Wife."

I am sure that we will all agree that there are bound to be a certain number of differences in wedded life; there will be quarrels at times. After all, two rational people, with minds of their own, will not always be in wholehearted agreement. The road of matrimony may not always be smooth, but it should be one in which husband and wife walk hand in hand, in the same direction, and with the same goals and purposes in mind. For, there are certain fundamentals of life that form the basis for a strong home life, and they cannot be compromised.

PARENT SUBSTITUTES

There are men who dream of marrying a girl "just like the girl that married dear old Dad." They want someone who can make pies just like the ones that "mother used to bake." Such husbands make a poor risk for marriage, because they are not really looking for a wife, but a substitute for their mother. They have not really broken with mother's apron strings.

There are wives who will tell you how good they had it at home, because Dad was such a good provider; he was always helping with the dishes and taking care of the children. They want a husband who will follow the same pattern. Maybe they are looking for a substitute for a father, but hardly for a husband.

This is an unwholesome attitude toward marriage. It is sometimes encouraged by parents, particularly by mothers who say at the wedding of their daughter, "I am not really losing a daughter, I am gaining a son." I am always afraid of that attitude, because a mother might just as well admit that she is losing a daughter.

Marriage is not supposed to be a substitute for parents upon whom we have become dependent. It is a partnership of two people, and meant to be a new, a different relationship. Overly dependent partners in marriage will most likely have a great many problems.

Sometimes wives will say, "All my husband wants is a housekeeper and a mother for his children." Husbands will reply, "All my wife wants is to have financial security." Now, there may be cases where this is true. But generally such remarks indicate an immature emotional attitude toward family life. There is a sense of wanting, instead of giving.

MATURE EXPECTATIONS

The emotionally mature person loves persons and uses things. The immature person loves things and uses people. In family life we are required both to give and to take in an emotional way. If it is always giving and never taking, we have become a slave instead of a marriage partner. If it is always taking and never giving we have become overly domineering.

There must be adjustments of one to another. We must be ready to accept our mates as they are, rather than as we always would like to have them be. When we set out into this adventure with the idea of making the other partner over into our own image and desires, we have a very poor basis for a strong marriage.

Some are always comparing their own marriage to other couples. They feel that others are better suited to each other, more loving and more happy. But the fact is that we do not know all the "ins and outs" of other people's lives. It has happened that the people whom we thought so ideally mated, were also envious of others whom they considered to be more happily married.

We also tend to carry over the spirit that was found in the home of our own parents. If they quarreled a good deal, this spirit may well carry over into our own homes. If there was a tender loving relationship, this also can be seen in the next generation.

ODIOUS COMPARISONS

But comparisons are hard to make, and always a bit odious. They also profit little in making marital adjustments in our own homes.

I do not believe that all handicaps in marriage are immediately overcome by faith. A girl who has been overly protected in her early life, is not just going to become a strong mature person because she has accepted Christ as her Savior. A person who has suffered rejection in early life is also going to carry this over into later life, even if he has a true faith in Christ.

We live on two levels. On the horizontal level we are going to be confronted by constant emotional and mental adjustments. If we are emotionally immature, we will carry this over into later life, even as Christians.

But we also live on a vertical line. And there is nothing that can strengthen the marriage bond more than the feeling of the living presence of God in our homes. The love between two people that is hallowed by a mutual love for God is the strongest bond of love.

So, for the Christian home, the adjustments that must be made between husband and wife become victories when there is the upward look. If we commit ourselves to God, we are in a far better position to give a complete commitment to our marriage partner. This strengthens the tie that binds in Christian love.

3. Tensions in the Home

INCREASING PRESSURE

There is something thrilling about a wedding. The beauty of the ceremony, the pledging of the vows, the nuptial caress, the kneeling couple, these all impress us with the blessings of a Christian family. But when I perform such a ceremony I cannot help but wonder how the atmosphere will be in that family one year, or five or ten years later. So often people say, "We get along well together; we have no more quarrels than the average couples have."

In a way this is a sad indictment. It is taken for granted that there will be tensions and that a good quarrel is inevitable now and then. The fact is that the family is the world's most powerful agency. When God chose to keep alive the spiritual line, he chose to do this through the agency of the family. The parent-child relationship is the greatest force in molding the lives of all of us.

Today the home is under an ever increasing amount of pressure. There are pressures from the community, from the school, from our work, and even from the church. It is usually the home that must adjust its schedule to meet the varying needs of these other agencies. These are facts that we must face realistically.

But the real tensions in the home come not so much from without as from within the family. They are related to the psychological conflicts that arise from our own behavior, our own feelings, or our relationship with people outside of the family circle. But the family often bears the brunt of it.

EXAMPLES

I can best illustrate this by citing a few examples. Johnny comes home from school. He has had a bad day. His ball team lost its game. The teacher had to discipline him for misbehaving. He also saw another boy walking his favorite girl friend home from school. So he comes home in an ugly mood. While he was on the playground he was a good sport; he even joked about his girl friend. But when he comes to the place where he can freely express his feelings he really lets go. He fights with his sister, he is disrespectful to his mother, he kicks the dog, and he generally shows the hostility he has in his heart.

This is a common occurrence. Someone speaks about such children being, "street angels but home devils." It is not reasonable to act that way, but few of us are reasonable when it comes to expressing our feelings. Fortunately many parents understand these reactions in their children and deal with them accordingly.

But now father comes home. His boss has not been too easy on him at the shop. He came to his car and found that one of the tires was flat. The traffic on the way home was very annoying. But he takes all this in fairly good grace, until he comes home. Then he takes out all his resentment on his family. The children are too noisy to suit him. The supper is not to his liking, and so he takes out his feelings on his wife.

The mother in the home may be in a similar mood. She takes out all the complaints of the day on her husband and children. When people meet in the unrestrained setting of the home under such circumstances, there will undoubtedly be some real tensions.

We often have subtle ways of suppressing our hostilities for a while, and then we transfer them to others, often to those we love best. A man cannot express his resentment to his boss; he might get fired. A boy cannot express his jealous feelings to his friends; they would laugh at him. So the home becomes the place where we love the most and treat our associates the worst.

Actually, such family members are acting on a very immature level. These are actually unhealthy reactions, and they can lead to serious consequences. Such things break down the morale of the family and tend to undermine the spiritual fiber of the home. Under such a situation the family altar loses its fire.

THE REMEDY

The remedy evidently lies in trying to take a more mature outlook on life. There are better ways of expressing resentment and hostility. But above all we must learn to look upon life's frustrations and disappointments not as stumbling blocks in the way, but stepping stones that lead to spiritual progress. The mature man has learned to deal constructively with life's irritations.

The emotionally mature man is one who has learned to find more satisfaction in giving than in receiving. He has learned the meaning of unselfish love. When the love in the home is hallowed by a love for Christ, it gains a new dimension. It is evident not only on a horizontal plane, but also on a vertical one. This is the great blessing of a Christian home.

Many of the tensions in the family would be resolved if we would act like mature men and women. The Bible has a good deal to say about developing spiritual maturity. But you never find it in people who are emotionally immature. It requires that we "put away childish things," also childish attitudes.

The best remedy I know for childishness is to become childlike, in the presence of the Lord of heaven and earth, also the Lord of the home. A common allegiance to Him, a mutual bowing before His will, and a united, heartfelt prayer brought to His throne, bind our families together with lasting bonds of love.

4. Changing Patterns in Home and Family

Much of the writing and speaking about home and family shows a rather naïve desire to have today's family remain just as it was in 1900. The picture of the traditional Christian home of that era is an attractive one, but we tend to forget that, with the changing times, there have also been changes in the family.

The breakdown of the old-fashioned home has not happened overnight. It has been the result of a long procession of events.

A man's home is not like a castle, with a drawbridge that can be lowered over a moat to allow the outside world to enter only when he will. The walls that separate us from the outside have become very thin, sometimes even transparent. There is a constant flow of influence that comes from the culture of the age in which we live.

INDUSTRIALIZATION OF SOCIETY

One of the changes that has greatly influenced the family circle is the movement toward industrialization of our society. People have moved to the cities in an ever larger number. This brings a changed atmosphere into the home, differing widely from the rural social order of some six decades ago. People live on 60-foot lots instead of 160-acre farms.

Life on the farm also has changed. The farmer has become a man who is engaged in a business venture with many records to keep, business deals to carry out, and government documents to be filed in triplicate. In addition to this, in the last decade the farm population has declined by five million, while the total population increased by nineteen million. In the 1800's some 64 per cent of our families lived on farms; in 1960 only 12 per cent live on farms.

With the changing developments in rural areas, farm families are no longer isolated units living by themselves. They have become fully as much a part of modern culture as have their city cousins. They also have their radio, TV, and daily papers. Their young men and women have the same education, and many enter into professions.

PROMOTING FAMILY UNITY

All of this increased industrialization has required a change in family living. The vast majority of people have separated their work from their homes. The family is no longer a team working at the same industrial enterprise, but members find employment in various fields. The result is that many members of the family are not at home for the noon meal, and some are not at home for the evening meal. It is a rare occasion when all the members of the family are at home for an entire evening.

In our present world, which is governed by the factory whistle, the scheduled appointments, or the hours of education, the family ties are being loosened, and the home is forced to adapt. It will do little good to long for the "good old days." But the situation does call us, as Christian families, to consider our new responsibility in our modern culture. For the home is still the most important unit in society, in the church, and in the line of God's way of working.

How, then, can we best promote the warm and loving spiritual atmosphere that is needed to make the home fulfill its important function? We may not allow the fires of the altar to go out, but this will naturally require some adjustments on our part.

If, for example, the family cannot get together for meal-time devotions regularly, would it not be well to find another time of day for family devotions? Will it not be of greater importance to stress the need of personal devotions by each member of the family? Should we, then, not be seriously seeking to promote a warm Christian atmosphere in which the children of today can become stalwart men and women of faith?

5. Lost Authority in Our Homes

The second Sunday in May is Mother's day. It is a day that is widely celebrated in our land. Mother is loaded with presents and praise, which she justly deserves.

The third Sunday in June is Father's day. This, too, is celebrated, but mostly by merchants who manage to use it as a time to sell ties and shirts for father. Somehow or other, not as much emotional warmth is packed into this celebration as the one for mother.

I call attention to this, not out of a spirit of envy or neglect, but because this shows a growing trend in the home and family today. Father is receding more and more into the shadows, while mother is becoming the more dominant figure in the family.

FATHER'S DECREASING ROLE

Since father is away from home a good deal of the time, the mother naturally carries on a major role in the training of the family. But there is a danger that "dear old dad" is looked upon more as a provider for the family than the head of the house.

The concept of a strong authoritarian figure in the home is slipping. This has been noted by many writers. I have clippings from magazines on this subject bearing such titles as, "Is the American Male a Man or a Mouse?" "Trousered Women and Dishwashing Fathers," "Should Husbands do Housework?" The changing role of the father deprives the family of a head who represents authority.

There are some writers who feel that this is just as it should be. They stress that a father must be a pal to his youngsters, and in this way establish their feelings of confidence in him. There can be no doubt that a stern and rejecting type of authority figure in the home is fraught with real emotional dangers. When children are afraid of father, there is a danger that they can develop a feeling of being rejected.

LACK OF AUTHORITY

But the opposite is also true. If there is no authority figure in the home, where will the children ever learn to respect authority? This is one of the reasons why some children rebel against their teachers, their leaders, and even the law.

Scripture clearly teaches that the father is the head of the house. In our marriage form the bride promises to "love, honor, and obey" her husband "in all things lawful." This is more than is demanded of some children. To be sure, the father is still regarded as the "head" of the family. But headship has come to mean something quite different from what it was a half century or more ago.

The growing trend today is toward the ideal of having father and mother assume the headship of the family as a joint venture. In this situation, since the mother is at home the greater part of the time, she assumes a more important role in this respect. The father then recedes into the background. To say that this is bad is an over-simplification. I know of some families where it is better that the mother plays a more dominant role than the father. In other families the father should play a more dominant role than the mother.

The important matter is that the children can feel that the parents together provide an atmosphere that reveals loving and understanding acceptance, but that at the same time acknowledges the parental authority our Lord requires. When there is a mutual acknowledgment of the supreme authority of our heavenly Father, there will be fewer problems concerning human authority. For these must blend together in every Christian home.

6. Christianity in the Home

The family is a place where emotions run especially deep. They affect the relationship between father and mother, between the parents and each child, and between the children among themselves. It is a place where there are frequent conflicts, and where forgiveness is frequently necessary. It is a place where we must put our Christian faith into practice in a far more intimate way than in any other place in life.

Since the family is also the basic unit for Christian nurture, the spiritual influences reach from one generation to the next.

SPIRITUAL INFLUENCES

But this is done in far more subtle ways than parents often realize. It is not just done by talking to children about religion, or by reading the Bible and by prayer. This is all very important and forms an essential part of family life. But Christian faith is revealed far more effectively in the interrelationship between parents and children.

For example, we teach our children to think of God as our heavenly Father, according to Scripture. But the word "father" has a specific meaning for a child, one that corresponds to the concept he has of his earthly father. If he pictures his own father as being stern and rejecting, one who often loses his temper, he is likely to gain the same picture of his heavenly Father.

We often see people with deep-seated feelings of guilt. They may have committed some outstanding sin in their earlier days, and find it hard to accept the forgiving love of God in Christ. However, you will usually find that such people have the basic problem that they are not able really to forgive themselves. They continue to chastise themselves because of what they have done and do not learn to "forget the things that are behind."

DEVELOPING GUILT FEELINGS

As a rule, such guilt-laden individuals have not experienced much forgiveness on a human level in their childhood days. They were punished in a rejecting sort of way – parents would indicate that they were ashamed of them for what they had done and that they were disappointed in having such a son or daughter.

Parents who use words such as "If you don't like it, you can get out," or, "You need never darken my door again," are setting the stage for serious emotional problems.

There are other illustrations that could serve to show the importance of putting Christian faith into practice in the home. Christian nurture is more than words, it is part of living together. And in this world of sin we are all fully aware of our own weaknesses, and should be willing to admit them even to our children. It should not be hard for a parent to say to his child, "I'm sorry." This does not undermine parental authority, but strengthens it.

GREAT RESPONSIBILITIES

The changing patterns in our homes have some tremendous implications for us as Christian parents. They load us with almost frightening responsibilities. The tremendous increase in emotional, mental, and spiritual breakdowns in children and young people show that we are not creating a healthy climate in our Christian homes, not as healthy as it should be.

The vocation of parenthood may at times be at variance with our personal concern for individual success and advancement; it may mean personal sacrifice, but it is a vocation that we dare not ignore. If we see our own families as part of God's people in his covenant relationship, we are fulfilling life's greatest task when we strive to carry out His will in our homes.

7. Too Young to Marry

In recent years there have been many young people who marry at an early age. Statistics have shown that this is always true when economic conditions are at a higher level. Young people can feel they are financially independent when they are seventeen or eighteen, and they set up a home with the concept that two can live as cheaply as one.

In some cases this is due to a forced marriage. An ever increasing number of young people must drop out of high school to take up home making. This indicates a growing laxity in the moral lives of our teen-agers. It is a situation that is beset by many dangers and implications for the home.

It must be said to the credit of many of the young people who have married at such an early age that they have made a marvelous adjustment to wedded life and have established a stable home that is a credit to the church and the community.

IMMATURE PARENTS

But there are many others who have not succeeded so well. It has been well established that more early marriages end up in divorce than marriages of young people over twenty-one. It stands to reason that there will be a certain amount of instability in homes in which parents themselves are only teen-agers.

Usually the husband and father, due to his age, is not able to find the best kind of employment. The wife and mother is often poorly equipped to run a home and finds the routine of managing a family rather boring and difficult. In our culture, young people of seventeen or eighteen are still somewhat immature in their reactions, so that there are frequent quarrels and conflicts that are resolved in an immature way.

It is little wonder that often children reared in such homes have emotional problems, for they live in an atmosphere that is unstable and immature.

YOUTHFUL GRANDPARENTS

There is a second danger that results from early marriages. These youthful parents will also, most likely, be youthful grandparents.

We often meet people who are grandparents at forty. Their children are growing up, they have more leisure time on their hands, but they are not quite ready to sit down and retire. In fact, they are still vigorous and strong, physically attractive and youthful looking. They have not reached the middle years of life.

So a youthful grandfather is active in bowling and other sports, as well as the activities of the church. The youthful grandmother finds employment as an outlet for her excess energies. The largest percentage of working mothers are in this class. They are cast out into the world of industry, business, or service organizations.

This presents a definite hazard. Too many in this age bracket find the temptations too great and they fall into relationships that lead to unfaithfulness to the marriage partner. They have not had a long period of youth, since they married at an early age, so they have their fling when the opportunity presents itself.

EARLY DATING

The answer to this situation is to encourage young people not to marry at such an early age. It is not good practice for young people to "go steady" when they are still in junior high or the early years of high school. Children at that age should be encouraged to go out in groups, or to "double," so that they do not take their love affairs too seriously. For early marriages do not just happen, they are the result of early dating and steady relationships.

But when young people marry at an early age, it is important that they avoid the pitfalls of such marriages. Gather up all the spiritual resources to make a stable home. Marriage is an achievement, it doesn't just happen. It is only when young people marry "in the Lord" that a truly Christian home and family can be established.

8. Should Mothers Seek Employment?

A few days ago I had occasion to dial the telephone number of one of the members of our church. A rather pathetic young voice answered, "No, Daddy isn't home yet. My mother is working, and I have to take care of the family till Daddy gets home." The little lad was obviously not very happy about his circumstance.

Such is the situation in an ever larger number of our homes. It has contributed a great deal towards the growing instability of our families. In 1890 only 14 percent of the total female working force was composed of married women, and only a small number of these were mothers. By 1960 there were more married women employed than single women.

Between 1940 and 1950 the number of employed mothers increased by 350 per cent. Today six and one half million mothers of children under eighteen are in the United States labor force. Some predict that soon the number of working mothers will exceed those who do not work away from home.

NOT CONDEMN ALL WORKING MOTHERS

I am sure no one would condemn in a wholesale way the fact of the working mother. There are many of them who are filling important positions in industry and in other fields. We gratefully acknowledge the contributions they are making.

But this is a matter that does require careful examination, for there are inherent dangers to the structure of the home when mother goes out to work. This can be a serious emotional hazard for the family. The proper care of an average family is a full-time job, and it would be a serious error to look upon it as only a part-time hobby.

Why do mothers work in positions outside the home?

Various reasons are given, but the basic one is to increase the family income. Often it is not a matter of need, but a desire to seek a higher status of living. The extra income enables the family to obtain things that could not be purchased with one pay check. It may well lead to a greater financial and material security for the family — but the absence of mother from the home can also lead to greater emotional insecurity.

DORDT COLLEGE
LIBRARY
Sioux Center, Iowa

INCREASED TENSIONS

When both father and mother work, the family life must be geared to the schedule of two people who work outside the home. This puts much pressure on family life. It often leads to increased tensions between the members of the family. Holding down two jobs also makes the mother extremely busy so that she has little time to spend with her family or in the extra things that make family life attractive.

The first responsibility of the mother is to her family. The role of the mother in bringing children into the world, and nurturing them in the fear of the Lord, remains her primary one. This is life's most important contribution. Buying a better house, nicer furniture, and more expensive gadgets cannot give emotional security to a growing youngster. He needs the presence of a mother and father who show love and acceptance.

When the material things are stressed excessively, the family begins to center about them. This forms a very poor basis for family living.

CAREFUL EXAMINATION

Each working mother should carefully examine her role in life. If her work undermines the emotional health of her family, it is doubtful whether she is making a constructive contribution to the home by bringing in extra cash. If it affects her own health – physically, emotionally, or spiritually – she should not take employment outside the home.

Each Christian family should consider this matter carefully, in the presence of the Lord. They should ask the question, "Is it really worth while?" For no family "can live by bread alone."

22787

9. A House — or a Home?

The modern house is a marvel of convenient living. Tremendous advances have been made in design to fit the needs of the modern family. The houses are lighted, heated, and gadgeted in a way that our fathers never dreamed of. No longer need we struggle with clinkers, split wood, or carry out ashes to give comfort and heat. Once a year we move the dial and, provided we pay the oil or gas bill, constant heat is maintained with no further effort.

With pushbutton ease the laundry is washed automatically, rinsed a half dozen times, and electrically dried. We often wonder how our mothers were able to do their work without benefit of electricity, refrigeration, and frozen foods. Instant mixed and prepared foods also have made the work much easier.

It is quite evident that in the American world there is a decided increase in the breakdown of the home and of family life. The increased divorce rates, the increase in problem children and young people, give ample evidence of this tragic fact. The foundation-stone of society is crumbling.

COMFORTABLE FAMILY LIVING

But is the matter so different in Christian circles? For many of us, too, live in a house rather than in a home. It is a place where the family lives, rather than a place for family living. The home is under an increasing amount of pressure from the outside. There are pressures from the community, from the school, and even from the church. There are many activities that lead the members of the family away from the family circle. We are busy coming and going, but there are few times when all are met together at one time.

It is usually the home that must adjust its schedule to these outside forces. The family often bears the brunt of situations that develop outside the home. This tends to break down strong family ties.

But the home is the most important link in the chain of development of children and young people. In fact, it forms the heart of the spiritual life for each member. For in the home setting are molded the spiritual values that form such important elements in Christian personality.

Teachers in school well know that when there is a breakdown in the home, it will become evident in the child in the school setting. Pastors know full well that when the family fails to fulfill its rightful place, the church also will suffer. We still count the strength of our congregations in the number of families, rather than in the number of individual members.

MENTAL HEALTH IN HOME

Another dangerous by-product of the breakdown of the family is the effect it has upon the mental health of the members of the family. Parents who drift apart lose some of the security and stability they need in the face of life's responsibilities. Children who do not receive the molding influence of a well-organized home life will suffer emotionally more than many realize. I am convinced that one reason for the large increase in admission of children and young people into mental hospitals is the instability of the home.

We all need a place to which we can withdraw from the rush of life, a place that we can call home. But home is more than a house, for the warmth of a hearth is not enough; we need the warmth of loving companionship and acceptance. We need a place where we will be understood and loved and where we can show our love. For each of us has a deep need both to love and to be loved.

It is our conviction that the basic foundations for mental health must be laid in this setting. Since the home is the basic unit of society, and the basic unit of the church, when the home becomes only a house, we lose something vital.

Just as the wheel needs a hub, so also the home needs God as the center about which each member gathers. It takes this kind of living to make a house a home. It requires a love that is hallowed by our love for Him.

10. Cold War in the Home

The state of the American home is not a very healthy one. There is an ever increasing number of marriages that end up in the divorce courts. There are many families who say they do not believe in divorce, or they do not want to break up for the sake of the children, so they hang together in a continual state of incompatibility. I am sure that most pastors have helped to patch up such disputes and have gone home wondering whether it would be a greater sin for these people to separate than to live together in the spirit of anger and hostility.

CRACKED HOMES

But there are also many families where there are no open hostilities; father and mother do not shout at each other with angry words, or throw things at each other, but they live in a continual state of cold war. The members of the family tolerate each other, but there is little love that cements the home into a strong unit of society or of the church.

John A. Schindler observes in one of his many popular writings, "The family is our number-one cause of disease." He is thinking especially of emotionally induced illnesses and disturbances of emotional adjustment in children.

It is quite evident that a home life that is charged with the spirit of a cold war is not exactly a healthy place to live, either for parents or for growing youngsters. There is usually a critical atmosphere that prevails, which is expressed in various ways. Sometimes biting criticisms are given to another member of the family who is addressed as "Honey." Sometimes sharp barbs are presented, but they are covered up with what is supposed to be a humorous remark.

Often the critical attitude begins with father or mother. This soon spills over to the children, and soon the whole atmosphere is filled with hostile criticisms. Each one tells the other what is wrong with him.

INFLUENCE ON CHILDREN

It is not surprising that when a child is brought up in such an atmosphere he will turn cynical and critical by the time he is ready to leave home. Home was never a very pleasant place anyway. As he leaves, he may not only rebel against the family, but also against all that the family stands for.

It is a strong statement that the family is the number-one cause of emotionally induced illnesses, but there is a great deal of evidence to substantiate this today. This does not mean that when there is an emotionally disturbed child we may point the finger of scorn at his parents. It is well to remember that parents also have parents, and that parents are part of the same cultural structure in which we share. There is little room for a holier-than-thou attitude when it comes to training children.

But it need not be so. The family can also be the number-one factor in producing emotional health. Living together as a family should not be looked upon as a problem, for it can be one of the greatest joys on earth. When there is a bond of love that links the family into a solid unit, it is one of the most glorious experiences. We all need to love and to be loved. We need those with whom we can share both our joys and our sorrows, for this enriches all of life's experiences.

A PLACE FOR EACH MEMBER

But then we must make our homes places where every member of the family likes to be. He must feel that here is a place where he is always welcome and accepted. It need not be an elaborate house or one that is lavishly furnished, but it needs the furnishings of a loving smile and the warmth of understanding.

The greatest contribution that can be made to growing youngsters is that they learn to love and to accept love. Where can this be found but in the home? It is for this reason that the choice of a life's mate is so very important. This should not be based simply on physical attraction, but on the basis of a love that is strong enough to weather the storms that lie ahead.

When this love is hallowed by a common love for God, it gives a firm basis for a home in which there is no room for a cold war. This is the healthiest setting for living and for nurturing our children – God's children.

11. Healthy Family Relationships

A young husband who was having considerable difficulty in his marriage said, "I didn't know that when I married I also married my wife's relatives." He should have known better, for when we marry we always marry into a family circle. We must also take this family circle "for better or for worse." But this often does produce some deep-seated problems in the family structure.

Some families have a very healthy relationship within the circle. They see each other often and find help and strength from each other's companionship and friendship. Other families meet out of a sense of duty, and these family gatherings are only continued as long as the father or the mother are still with them.

THE FAMILY CIRCLE

There are other family circles in which there is a great deal of rivalry and often open warfare. It would seem that there is often more reason for strife between the in-laws than between brothers and sisters. Often jealousy — due to the fact that one is more prosperous than the other — underlies these hostilities. This can lead to most unpleasant situations.

The mother-in-law has been the object of many unkind remarks and crude jokes. Parents-in-law can be a help, but also a hindrance, to a good marriage in the family. Too much interference on the part of parents can lead to severe emotional problems in a young family. It's only natural that the husband or the wife will feel a greater allegiance to parents than to in-laws.

Parents should do all they can to enjoy their children in childhood and adolescence so that, when they marry, they can relinquish them to their mates. The success of any marriage requires that husband and wife may be able to live their own lives, fight their own battles, and face their own frustrations. Many misguided efforts at helpfulness turn out to be a burden to the young married couple. Parents should make a determined effort to stay out of the lives of their married children.

A HEALTHY INDEPENDENCE

This is but part of the process of the growing independence of a child. When a child is young he is the most dependent of all the creatures, and he remains so much longer than other creatures. But, as the child grows, an important part of his development is that he learns to make his own decisions and to stand on his own feet. A "mamma's boy" makes a poor risk for marriage.

Parents are best accepted by their in-laws when they learn to allow them to work out their own problems. Parents should be able to complete the training of their children by the time they are ready for marriage. If this is not true, either the young people are too young to marry, or the parents have not been willing to let their youngsters grow up.

The lion and the wolf teach their cubs to hunt for food. The eagle painfully pushes the young fledglings out of the nest so that they may learn to fly. But parents often want to cling to their children as if they think themselves indispensable.

Some children give in to this spirit of their parents, allowing the parents to dominate their lives and to help them in various ways. The married daughter will always have a listening ear whenever she has a quarrel with her husband, or she can "go home to mother" when the going gets rough. This leads to many emotional difficulties in such a family.

Other children rebel against parental interference. They find it hard to accept the watchful eye of doting parents or the critical remarks of an in-law. This, too, has produced disastrous results in young families.

If we have been wise enough to instill within our growing children a respect for abiding principles, and have built upon spiritual foundations, we can rejoice in their independence, for this will bring out the best in them. If we fear their independence, we have not done our work of training well.

Mutual understanding is important for healthy family relationships. A spirit of Christian concern and helpfulness will aid in creating an atmosphere of goodwill and love which must be the foundation stone for all family living.

12. In Defense of Mothers-in-law

The term "mother" speaks of one of the tenderest and most beautiful human relationships. This name has the power to stir up some of the sweetest memories and is the most frequent word on the lips of little children. But this tender word loses some of its winsomeness when it becomes "mother-in-law." Many jokes are told at her expense, and often these bits of crude humor have sharp barbs in them.

Why should this be so? The fault is partly her own, but it is surely not hers alone. She has often been sinned against as much as sinning. Her situation is more trying than that of father-in-law, because her contacts are more intimate. But it is a matter that has many dangers in it, for it has often contributed to the unhappiness of a married son or daughter. True, this is usually due to a lack of tact, thoughtfulness, or understanding, rather than a deliberate attempt to sabotage the marriage or to make the lives of her children miserable.

MOTHER AND MOTHER-IN-LAW

To be a mother-in-law, a woman must first be a mother. And she remains the same person in either role. But there is a difference in these two roles. The role of a mother-in-law is a very delicate and sensitive one. She is called upon to be a mother to one who is really not her own. She has to exercise a love that can hide a multitude of weaknesses, and there are countless women who carry out this responsibility with beautiful success. It is not unusual for in-laws to regard the mother-in-law with affection equal to that for a mother.

But this is not always the case. Sometimes a successful mother makes a blundering mother-in-law. When a mother has become intensely attached to a son or daughter, she will find it hard to give her offspring into the arms of another, and to allow them to function without parental interference.

This becomes especially difficult when the son or daughter has become a bit overly dependent on mother and so finds it hard to break the tie with mother. But to have a successful marriage, this must take place.

It is not wise for married children to live in with the parents, or even to live next door to them. It is extremely difficult to avoid interference in family affairs when parents and children live too close. Some sons-in-law or daughters-in-law interpret every suggestion as an invasion of their privacy, and feel deeply threatened by it.

A NEW RELATIONSHIP

Some mothers-in-law feel deeply disturbed when a new son-in-law or daughter-in-law does not show the same love and respect that they receive from their own children. But why should they feel this way? This is a new relationship, it's a different role, and it will always take time and patience to develop strong family ties.

This situation calls for a genuine spirit of understanding on the part of all concerned. If each one can approach this new relationship with a common-sense appreciation of the other's attitudes and problems, it can lead to a wholesome situation, one that can enrich the lives of all concerned.

Parents have a right to expect a measure of respect from all their children, whether they have been born to them or whether they have received them through marriage. But parents must also make themselves worthy of the respect and love of all their children.

This will require a mature approach to marriage and the family involvement in marriage. Young people may well consider that they do not just marry the girl or the boy they love, but they also enter into a new family circle. This is an added argument against mixed marriages.

One of the most beautiful illustrations of a warm and loving relationship between a mother-in-law and a daughter-in-law is that of Naomi and Ruth. They were knit together with strong ties that became stronger in days of sorrow and poverty. But it was a relationship that was cemented together by a common faith in God. This is always the soundest basis for life's most tender and enduring relationships.

13. The Common-sense Approach

When a person is faced with a difficult problem, a well-meaning friend will often give the advice, "All you need to do is use a little common sense." This kind of suggestion is only partially true. Common sense is important in handling the problem, in analyzing the situation and knowing what to do about it. But often things are not what they seem on the surface, and for that reason they require more than common sense. It is also true that common sense is rather uncommon.

The term "common sense" originally referred to the ability of man to unite the impressions of all the five senses. But it has come to mean practical judgment, or just ordinary good sense. It is something that is not taught but that is developed as a person matures, and some people never seem to have a great deal of it.

Some people have stated that all that psychiatrists and professional therapists do is to make use of common sense. Though it is true that a good measure of common sense is important for a therapist, he does far more than this. He will not base his judgments on the facts that lie on the surface but will delve more deeply into the underlying causes and drives. He deals with the more basic elements of the human personality.

SNAP JUDGMENTS

Things are not always what they seem to be to the casual observer. Some people are so ready to give simple answers to the problems of others. To them a matter is as clear as day because they make their opinions on the things they observe, or they compare with others who have had similar symptoms.

A wife states that she cannot get along with her husband and that she feels they will have to separate. It would seem on the surface that they are incompatible. The conclusion is readily made that the mistake occurred when this girl chose her husband. But further investigation shows that this girl would have had the same problems if she had married a different man, for she is not well-equipped emotionally for marriage.

A man cannot hold a job and shifts from one position to another.

Some people conclude that he is shiftless and a poor worker. But a closer scrutiny of the situation reveals that this man's instability springs from his childhood and the training he received in early life.

A boy of twelve gets caught stealing some money. On the surface it would seem that he needs money for one purpose or another, and so steals. The facts show that he stole, and arranged to get caught, in order to gain more attention, and this was the only way he knew how to get it.

UNCONSCIOUS MOTIVATIONS

Things are not always what they seem on the surface. It is important to look for unconscious motivations that underlie the actions and attitudes of others.

I know there are some who feel that too much emphasis is laid upon the psychological and the unconscious factors in man and that, as a result, we no longer acknowledge the real sinfulness of the human heart. Some will say, "Sin is sin, no matter how you look at it." This is true, but it is also true that there are often psychological backgrounds to the sinful actions of men.

Sometimes members of church councils are called upon to make judgments about the acts of people, whether they should be treated as sinners or as people who have a problem. These are sometimes difficult decisions to make. But in such matters it would be wise to determine first if there are psychological factors that enter into the sinful acts.

Often the common-sense approach is not enough. You need the guidance of those who have been professionally trained to make judgments in such matters. People often suffer at the hands and lips of the common-sense diagnostician who has a ready and simple remedy for a complicated problem. They can often do a great deal of harm by insisting on their helpfulness.

To be sure, make use of your good common sense, but mix your common sense with a genuine Christian understanding. We all need understanding, but there is no one who needs it more than the person who has emotional or mental problems. This, too, is an important ingredient of Christian love.

14. "There's No Place Like Home"

The home should be a place where people like to be. It should have that pleasant, inviting atmosphere that beckons us to come in. It is a sad thing when some members of the family would rather be away from the family circle. Many of our homes are being destroyed by this situation. It is up to us as parents to make the home a place where children enjoy living.

THE HOUSE

The arrangement of the dwelling should be such that it is livable. It need not be a mansion; in fact, many of the luxurious houses are not livable homes. The furnishings, too, should be adapted to the needs of the family, so that each member can enjoy living in it.

An excessive demand on neatness can destroy the usefulness of a house. Some mothers are inclined to stress this to an extreme. A boy was telling about the situation in his home, and mentioned that, when he came home from school with his books, he could not even lay them down for a few moments in the kitchen, but would immediately have to take them to his room upstairs.

Naturally, the opposite is also true. If the house is messy and unkempt, children will be ashamed to take their friends into the home. It is well to find a happy medium. I like to see a house that has that "lived-in" look, that gives the impression that this is the place where people live and feel at home.

The spirit that pervades the family is even more important. Many homes are destroyed by a great deal of scolding and rebuking. Sometimes this degenerates into a constant nagging when parents become so negative in their approach that they are constantly telling their children what they may not do. Such parents make it unpleasant for themselves and for their children. Often they use this as a means to let off steam and to express their feelings of hostility.

FAMILY DISCIPLINE

On the other hand, a home should not be undisciplined. Without discipline you cannot have a happy and well-regulated family. A child gains a measure of security when he knows what he may do and may not do. One writer described the condition in families that try to use an extremely permissive attitude towards the children as "striking only in self-defense."

Here, too, there must be a happy medium. Try to develop the spirit of *ich wil* rather than *du zollst.* The child must learn to take his place in the family because he feels that he is a member of the team, rather than because he is afraid of the consequences if he does not conform.

Too many "dos" and "don'ts" can ruin a home. When there are many regulations and laws, a family becomes an institution, and the father and mother are policemen who have to enforce the rules. No one likes to live in an institution. The spirit of living together on a level of mutual confidence must be fostered.

NEEDED COMMUNICATION

I find many young people who complain that they cannot talk over their problems with their parents. They feel that their parents will not, or simply do not, understand. This is not something that develops in adolescent years. If you keep the confidence of your child when he is still young, as he grows older he will continue to trust you.

This is a most important consideration, for often the more intimate things of life must be discussed. We all have problems, and the best way to conquer them is to find a listening ear and an understanding heart, and then pour out these problems. We should learn the art of listening, for this is basic to good mutual interrelationships also in the family circle.

When parents learn to accept their children as they are, with all their weaknesses and imperfections, children will also learn to accept their parents with their failings and shortcomings. In the family we see the lives of people most closely intertwined. If they are not bound together with the ties of love and mutual understanding, frictions drive them apart.

In fact, the real strength of the home is not first of all the family altar — even though this is most important — but it is the spirit of living together as Christians who recognize one Father and One Lord and King. There is no place like home to exercise this kind of Christian living.

PARENTS AND THEIR CHILDREN

And these words, which I command thee this day
shall be upon thy heart:
And thou shalt teach them diligently to thy children,
and shalt talk of them
when thou sittest in thy house,
and when thou walkest in the way,
and when thou liest down,
and when thou risest up.
And thou shalt bind them for a sign upon thy hands,
and they shall be for frontlets between thine eyes.
And thou shalt write them
upon the door-post of thy house
and upon thy gates.

Moses — Deuteronomy 6

15. You and Your Shadow

I have a little shadow that goes in and out with me,
And what can be the use of him, is more than I can see.

This little poem, which most of us can recall from childhood, has a good deal of truth concealed in its simple lines. For each of us has a shadow that goes with us wherever we go. It is the shadow of personal influence. This is not something that we can lay aside at times, and then put on again like a bit of clothing, but it is always with us. It is like the light that is shed by a lamp, like the heat that flows from a flame, like the fragrance of a flower.

It has a strange power upon the lives of others. Even when we are not fully aware of the fact, others do see us, hear us, observe us and their lives are touched by the influences that flow from us.

PERSONAL INFLUENCE

When the disciples saw their Lord in prayer, and observed the expression of his sinless face as He spoke to his Father, they were so moved that they asked him also to instruct them in the art of prayer. Often an expression of loving concern for others has served as an inspiration for others to follow and do likewise. Life is full of examples of men and women who have cast their shadow of personal influence upon the lives of others. Worthwhile and noble actions have been a blessing.

But the personal influence can be also an evil one. There are men and women in the entertainment world, who influence thousands of people, but their influence is often an unworthy one. They feed a spirit of sensuousness, materialism, and secularism. Others may cast their shadows in smaller spheres, such as a group of men working in a section of a factory, or a crew of construction workers, or possibly a few people in a neighborhood.

Even after death, the shadow will still be felt. We may think that we have lost our loved ones when we no longer see their faces or hear their voices, but the memory of pure lives may be more poignant after they have gone, for then we are inclined to forget their weaknesses. The influence of a godly father or a loving mother lives on in the lives of the children, sometimes even into the following generations.

Some men have cast long shadows on the history of the world, and the development of a nation. Others have cast their shadow in the realm of Christian thought or doctrine. Some have exerted their influence in art, or music, or literature. But whether the influence be great or small, each person casts his shadow. It is a question whether it be for good, or for evil.

PARENTAL INFLUENCE

There is no place in life where the personal influence is stronger than in the family line. Parents will influence their children, whether they want to or not. It is only a question of what kind of heritage they will leave with them.

It is not only a question of good and evil. Parents influence their children also through the emotional tone created in the home. When there are many tensions between the parents, or transferred from parents to children, these will also cast a shadow in which the children will walk, possibly all their days.

I sometimes get the impression from people that they feel that the spiritual blessings are transferred in some mysterious way from parents to children. This is not so. Each parent stands as a link in that chain, and it depends upon the influence, the sense of values, the spiritual tone that is passed on from one generation to the next.

The shadows we cast must ever reveal that we live in the greater shadow that Christ has cast upon our lives and upon our homes.

SPIRITUAL INFLUENCE

Many say today, "As long as I do what I feel is right, what do I care what others may think or say." It is true that we need not be a slave to public opinion. It is true also that the Bible teaches Christian liberty. But the Scriptures teach also that our liberty is limited by our influence upon others. Paul was not opposed to eating meat, but he said that he would never eat meat again, if it would be a stumbling block to the weaker brother.

You may be able to reconcile your conduct with your own conscience, but if it causes others to stumble, you cannot reconcile your conduct before God. Others are walking in your shadow, so we must ever beware of the influence that flows from your lives.

Jesus, in his earthly life, cast a great and abiding shadow, and the world has never been the same since He walked upon it. Walk then in the shadow of his abiding influence, and then the little shadows we cast upon our generation will help others to walk toward the place where there shall be no more shadows.

16. The Personal Touch

The rapid changes in contemporary living have brought our youth face to face with new problems and obstacles. Conditions over which we have little control make growing up more difficult than a generation ago. With the mounting population in our communities and our schools, relationships become more and more impersonal. Young people often search in vain for someone to understand them as an individual personality. We are losing the personal touch.

PARENTAL GUIDANCE

The home setting is still the ideal place for children to discuss their problems. Parents often feel that they are too busy to sit down to talk things over with their children. Some parents still try to carry out the old adage that "children should be seen and not heard." Such an attitude is by no means healthy for a youngster bursting with a desire for self-expression.

We need the art of listening also to the younger generation. If a child finds that he can talk things over with his parents in confidence, he will continue to do so also when he is older.

When a child comes home from school and says, "I hate my teacher," the natural impulse for parents is to say, "You may not say that; that is wrong, it is sinful." You may succeed in keeping him quiet, but it would be far better for the child if you would find out why he does not like his teacher on that particular day, when usually he likes her very much. Repeatedly repressing the feeling of a youngster will lead him on to the point where he will soon refuse to tell his parents about his feelings, and then he will take the attitude that they don't care anyway.

To develop a wholesome relationship does not mean that we have to pamper children, nor even that we have to be a "pal" to them. We remain father and mother, but at the same time we must be a guide and counselor. We must give firm guidance. They must know that there are certain lines they may not cross. But this is not gained by wielding the big stick of parental authority, but by gaining their deserved personal confidence.

GUIDANCE IN OUR SCHOOLS

Our growing school systems are often so busy with the regular routine of school life and all its incidentals that we lose sight of one of the greatest factors involved, that of the interpersonal contact between the teacher and the pupils.

It is generally not too difficult to teach the average, or the above average, youngsters, but what about those who have learning problems? What are we doing for those who are very shy, or those who are overly aggressive? Do our teachers have the time, or take the time, to deal personally with those who are not doing well? It is these who often get into trouble in later life. If we do little more than give punitive marks, we have missed one of the real goals of our school system.

In most of our schools we are making a beginning of testing programs. These can have great value, but they are also fraught with dangers. Not all teachers are able properly to interpret these testing results. And there is still the need for a person to person guidance.

I am convinced that some of the tragic breakdowns in the teenage years could be prevented if these children would have had the benefit of skillful professional counsel in their earlier years. But many parents are reluctant to seek such help outside of the school system, either because of the cost involved, or because they feel that there is a stigma attached to having their child see a psychologist or psychiatrist.

PASTORAL GUIDANCE

Many of our churches are suffering in the same way. Many pastors in large churches find it impossible to reach all their children and young people. It becomes a physical impossibility to conduct the various classes, and the result is a lessening of the interpersonal contact between pastor and the children of the church.

And yet, this is the age when pastoral counsel is greatly needed, possibly more than at any other time. It is during these first years of life that we hope to see life's greatest spiritual commitment. Children and young people stand at the fork of the road. The world lures them with all its splendid resources, while on the other hand the challenge of the gospel also reaches out to them.

To flounder at this age in life can lead to sad results for the years ahead. To gain spiritual as well as mental and emotional health, calls for the personal touch also of the pastor.

As Christians we possibly have the best opportunity to guide our children and young people into wholesome paths of Christian living. In principle, the home, the school, and the church unite together to make an impact upon the impressionable lives of our youth.

But are we really developing stronger, more consecrated young people? I wonder. I am afraid that we are in danger of losing the personal touch.

17. Controls — Internal or External?

Parents are constantly confronted with the question of discipline in the family. We want to keep our children on the straight and narrow path, but at the same time, we do not want to dominate their lives completely. We know there are times when they need discipline, and yet we do not want to be too authoritarian.

A lack of adequate discipline leads to insecurity for a child, for he will not learn to know the difference between right and wrong. Discipline that is too severe stands in the way of congenial family living, inhibits the child unduly, and often leads to rebellion.

Discipline is necessary for a well-regulated home. But it must always have as its purpose the welfare of the child and not be a means of giving a parent the satisfaction of getting rid of pent-up hostile feelings. It must be a means of control, and for the child it is a form of external control.

SOCIAL AND ETHICAL CONTROLS

Every person needs social and ethical controls, for we all have basic desires that must be governed and kept in check. If such desires were allowed free play, life would be impossible in our society. To keep these desires in proper channels, there must be some force that directs them and, at times, curbs them.

Today many of the codes of living that prevailed in a previous generation are no longer accepted. People do not like to be bound by rules and regulations, for they feel that life should be more permissive. This has led to some tragic results.

It is evident that, in children and immature persons, external controls are still needed. If you let your child freely express himself, without any controls, his self-expression is going to lead into some unwholesome channels. Children are conceived and born in sin. They do not have the emotional stability that enables them to handle their freedom.

This is also true for many adults. People living in slum areas usually need a great deal of external control, sometimes even forcefully applied. The police cruisers roam the streets and make frequent stops. Often the law must step in and clean up immoral conditions.

Even in our schools, teachers must be constantly on their guard to prevent cheating in examinations. All kinds of rules and regulations must be established to control the lives of young people living in dormitories. These are all external controls, and they are needed.

INNER CONTROLS

This is not the ideal. Since we live in a sinful world, we will always need some external controls. However, a mature person should also strive to develop inner controls. He should learn to bring his basic drives under the control of his own will, his conscience, and his sense of values.

This is something that does not come easily or painlessly. It must be taught from infancy on. It is part of the education of a child and the building of character. Discipline in the home must have this as part of its goal. Discipline establishes external controls so that, as time goes on, the developing person may learn to develop inner controls of his own.

A child may be beaten into submission when he is still young, but often this leads him to feel that, when he is too old to spank, he will still do as he pleases. He may be forced to do something against his will, but he is of the same opinion still. In such a case, discipline has failed.

Properly used, discipline is a means to help a young person develop to that stage where he can learn to control himself. Here the Christian faith offers an inner force that drives man to obey the demands of both God and man.

"Thy word have I laid up in my heart, that I might not sin against thee." This is the most powerful inner control a person can possess.

18. Should Johnny Be Spanked?

When I meet with parents' groups, such as PTA meetings or Mr. and Mrs. clubs, a favorite question for discussion concerns the use of corporal punishment. This subject seems to create a lot of guilt feelings in the minds of parents, either when they administer a spanking at times, or when they don't and feel that they should.

There is no hard and fast rule that can be laid down, nor is it possible to give a list of offenses that would require a spanking, and those that should not. There is considerable difference between children; for some such punishment is effective, for others it is not. It depends on how sensitive the child is, and how good the relationship is between parents and child.

In a previous chapter we mentioned that controls, either external or internal, must be placed upon every person. For a young child such controls must of necessity be external ones. When children are still young they do not understand language too well, but they do understand the meaning of a few taps gently administered in the right place and at the proper time.

IMPORTANCE OF ATTITUDES

If parents have to do a great deal of spanking, it would be well for them to examine their attitude toward their children. Frequent use of forcible means would indicate that parents are trying to be too strict, or they may have stirred rebellion in their youngsters. Possibly such parents are expressing their own hostilities toward their youngsters.

Discipline is part of habit training in children. It is not a matter of retribution or working off an annoyance. For that reason it should always be reasonable, fair, and just. Parents have been known to punish children severely for breaking a valuable vase. But a child could not possibly understand the value of such an object; for all he knew, it might have come from a dime store. This is an affront to the child's sense of justice.

A psychologist visiting a home noted that a great many commands were given to the children. According to his statistics, in a two-hour period seventy commands were given, twenty-three times they were told what to do, and forty-seven times they were told what not to do. If all these commands were to be enforced, a great deal of discipline would be needed. But it would be utterly useless.

Some parents feel that they must punish merely to assert their authority. They try to get their children to do things, which may have no real value for the child, but they must be done because mother, or dad, has said so. The child may not ask for reasons; he must just obey.

DELAYED PUNISHMENT

It is bad policy to delay punishment till daddy gets home. Many a child has learned to dread the arrival of his father in the evening, for fear that the offenses of the day will have to be settled. The punishment must be related to the crime, both as to its nature and its timing.

If children get the idea that discipline is a form of tyranny, or that both, or one, of the parents are tyrants, we have lost the true meaning of discipline. If children must be ruled by fear, we have lost one of the most precious elements in parent-child relationship, namely, love.

Spanking a child that is past his tenth year should be an extreme exception. If we cannot reason with our children by that time, all previous discipline has been utterly in vain. Other means of discipline, such as taking away a privilege, will be more effective at that time in life.

There is a place for discipline. Wise King Solomon said, "Withhold not correction from the child, for if thou beat him with a rod, he will not die." We may not neglect discipline, even though it is unpleasant. But it must always have as its purpose the breaking down of a bad habit, and the building of a good one.

Pray for the wisdom to use discipline wisely, to exercise it in love, and to make it fit into the spirit of a Christian home.

19. Christian Nurture and Maturity

One of the important goals in the training of our children, and in the development of our own lives, is to achieve greater maturity. We need to grow up so that we can get out of the "cry-baby" stage and become full-grown men and women. This will require that we develop adequate means of adjustment to our selves, to others, to our environment, and to God.

There is a definite relationship between emotional and spiritual maturity. It is hard to conceive of a person being emotionally immature and at the same time spiritually mature. There is a great deal of emotion in our religious life so that a person who has poorly controlled feelings will hardly be strong spiritually.

VARIOUS AGENCIES

Maturity can be achieved only by means of Christian nurture. The home, the school, and the church make their contribution to help us grow up. In early life the home is the greatest factor in training. During the school years the largest contribution to the developing personality is made by the teachers, and in and through all these agencies the church plays a great role.

The Christian home forms the ideal setting for developing the child in his formative years. The emotional life of a child is greatly influenced by the emotional tone of the family. Here a person learns how to face life with its frustrations in the way that is taught by the word and example of his parents.

The school takes its place alongside the home in this task. The goal is not just to fill the little heads with facts, but to teach the child to face life as it is in the world of today and possibly in the world of tomorrow.

The teaching role of the church plays its part in developing spiritual maturity. The truths of God and his Word are taught. But these truths are also applied to everyday living.

DISCIPLINE OF EXPERIENCE

In addition to these formal agencies, there is the nurture of the various experiences of life. A step in the maturing process is the developing of a skill in a field of labor, in management, or in one of the professions. Many learn great lessons also through the discipline of pain and illness and struggle.

But with all these means of Christian nurture we have been able to enjoy, why are there still so many of us who are childish in their attitudes toward life? Why are there so many who rate so low on the maturity scale?

I fear that often we have equated knowledge with maturity. We feel that when we have taken care of the intellectual side of our training, we have done our bit. We often leave the emotional side of life to take care of itself.

But even though we do cram our heads full of facts, we have not thereby achieved maturity. Knowledge alone does not make a successful man. We meet people who are very well educated, who have read widely and deeply, and who can use a great deal of psychological terminology — but they are poorly adjusted to life. They have knowledge, but they cannot make the grade.

IMPORTANCE OF EMOTIONAL FACTORS

The driving forces of life are emotional, rather than intellectual. Man is a thinking and rational being, but we are not as rational as we think we are. A person usually does not grow up to be a Protestant, a Catholic, or a Mohammedan, because he is convinced that his particular view of religion gives the most intelligent answers to life's questions and problems. He usually is a member of one of these groups because his parents were of that faith.

A person grows up to be truthful, honest, and generous, not because he is intellectually convinced that such virtues are best for him, but because he has seen these virtues in practice and precept in his home and cultural setting.

Conditions that favor a healthy emotional life must be provided to give the kind of Christian nurture that will lead to emotional and spiritual maturity. Have we possibly neglected the emotional side of life in our Christian culture, and thus developed many who are both emotionally and spiritually immature?

20. Motivation

"You can lead a horse to water, but you can't make him drink." This is also true in the world of people. Parents can send their children to school, but it is not always easy to make them study. Teachers are greatly concerned with motivation in the learning process. It is a well-known fact that a student learns only when he is motivated to learn. Giving poor marks or constantly telling a child to get to work is of little avail if a child is not motivated to learn.

REMOTIVATION TECHNIQUES

Motivation is also an important word in a mental hospital. The staff members frequently speak of trying to develop a greater desire in a patient to become well, or the urge to get back home and to work. Motivation and re-motivation techniques are employed as part of the treatment program.

In a recent pastors' workshop the discussion centered on a similar subject. Pastors are concerned with developing means that can motivate people to greater interest in the church and a greater desire to witness. In our affluent society, it is not easy to motivate young people to enter fields of kingdom work.

We all need to be motivated to carry out our regular obligations in life. There must be some force that makes us get up in the morning and that drives us to do our work and to try to live successful lives. Some people have more of this than others. Some are self-starters; others must be cranked. Usually it is the self-starters who are successful and make the greatest contribution to society and to the kingdom.

The things that motivate people differ widely. Some are motivated by things that are rather earthy and mundane. Andrew Carnegie once greeted a body of college students by saying, "I address myself only to those among you who have ambition to become millionaires." Greed for gold is a strong drive in all life's pursuits. If we did not have to work to make a living, most of us would live by quite a different schedule than we do.

LONGING FOR ACCEPTANCE

The longing for the esteem of our fellow men, for social acceptance, is also a strong drive in the majority of people in our culture. These are not the loftiest motivating forces, but they are sufficiently effective for some people.

Motivation is an emotional drive that rises from our feelings and our will. It is often stirred by the imagination. It is the energy within us that makes us reach out to worth-while goals. It is the power that can keep us going, even when the going is not easy. In addition to the inner urge, there is often some outer pressure. Our feelings alone are too unsteady; they need to have a stabilizing force from outside of us. Then it is not only a matter of "desire" but also the feeling of "ought."

INNER INCENTIVES

It is a well-known fact that just telling a person what he ought to do is not sufficient. It is not enough for parents merely to tell their children what they should do, and what they should not do. These words often have to be enforced with stronger incentives. A child must develop the inner incentive to do the things that are right and shun the things that are evil. In a succeeding chapter I would like to suggest how this can be done.

It is hard to overestimate the importance of attempting to instill worthy motivating influences in the lives of our children. This they will carry with them through all of life. When a child is young, force may be useful. But in the growing personality, something higher is needed. Parents must do all in their power to lead their children in this direction.

WORTHWHILE IDEALS

Setting a worth-while ideal is a great help in motivating a person. The desire to achieve such an ideal can be a strong force in life. When a young man has as his goal to become a medical doctor, he is willing to sacrifice much and to work hard to reach that goal. He will put his best into it. It is here that many high school students fall short. Because they do not have goals, they move aimlessly through the prescribed years. They lack direction, and hence also the power to move into that direction.

A person needs motivating power to live satisfactorily in this life. But he needs this even more in the spiritual life. The Christian faith holds before us the loftiest of ideals for our best efforts. These ideals are not just seen in facts and ideas, but they are seen in a living and loving Person. There can be no stronger power to motivate a man than to have as his goal "to be like Him."

21. How to Motivate Our Children

Mother says to Johnny, "You must get busy with your homework." Johnny says, "I don't feel like it." If mother is not able to change Johnny's feelings, he is not going to do much studying. Mother can force him to look at his books, but if he is not motivated, he is not going to learn much.

What are some of the things that motivate the actions of people, either children or adults? Merely reasoning or arguing with a person is not going to accomplish the desired results, for motivation is not an intellectual matter alone; it is also an emotional matter. It is not reasoning but attitudes that count. It is basically an emotional drive, an inner energy that urges us to reach worth-while goals.

POWER OF EXAMPLE

One of the most powerful forces in a child is that of example. A boy will tell his teacher, "Why should I study? My Dad never went beyond the eighth grade, and he is very successful." If the parents never read a book or study something worth while, it is quite possible that the children will not be much interested in study. The attitude and the actions of parents often speak much louder than their words.

It has been definitely proved that in the classroom the relationship between teacher and pupil has an important bearing on learning. If the pupil does not like the teacher, he will often reject what is taught. Studies show that a well-liked teacher makes for a well-liked subject.

This is also an important factor in the vocational choices of young people. If the minister is well accepted and he presents a favorable picture of the ministry in his own attitudes, a young man in the church is more likely to feel inclined to choose the ministry as a career. The lack of candidates for the ministry would indicate that our ministers have not always presented a favorable image of this important office.

USE OF RIVALRY

The Jesuit teachers, in addition to stressing a sense of duty, developed stimulation to study in their students by the use of rivalry. Pupils were often grouped with others of somewhat equal ability. Rival groups were placed in competition to stimulate learning. Honor societies serve as an incentive for many students today. Rivalry can be a powerful motivating force.

Lecturing and scolding a child seldom serves as a means of motivation. A genuine acceptance, coupled with the powerful means of appreciation and commendation, can accomplish far more. One little boy was a problem to his Sunday-school teacher. His behavior and interest in the class were not very good. The teacher made him secretary of the class with the responsibility of calling the roll and keeping the records. The lad suddenly changed, for he found what he needed – acceptance and appreciation.

PRACTICAL GOALS

Setting up worth-while and practical goals and ideals is always a good thing for any child. Every person needs some goal in life, for this makes life worth living. One of the worst diseases of our age is the lack of direction, the spirit of aimlessness and boredom evident in many young people. They don't know where they are going, and they don't particularly care. Why should they get an education when they have no objectives in mind?

I listened to a discussion on the "Role of Religion in Human Motivation." The discussion was rather disheartening, for the conclusion presented was that religion does not play such a great part in motivation as many people think. Only the small minority of people feel strongly motivated by religion. When their religion has touched every part of their lives, only then does it serve to stimulate to noble deeds, to lofty thoughts, and to "reach out toward the stars."

I began to wonder about the motivating faith in the church. We face a shortage of ministers, missionaries, nurses, doctors, psychologists, and social workers. Evidently, we still have a long way to go.

22. Roots and Wings

At one of the recent pastors' conferences, Dr. Stuart Bergsma, Superintendent at Pine Rest Hospital, made the telling statement that in the training of children parents should give them "roots and wings." This brief statement pictures the heart of the task we have as parents in our relationship with our growing youngsters.

It is important that children find solid roots for their lives while they are in the family setting. They need to find a sense of security, a feeling of confidence that will enable them to face life today and the world of tomorrow. The emotional atmosphere of the home is the creative factor that determines this.

MORAL ROOTS

They need moral roots, since they must know what is right and what is wrong. This will require loving guidance, careful discipline, and sincere effort on our part. Especially during the first five years of life this must be stressed, but this goes on as long as they are under the parental influence.

Children also need spiritual and cultural roots that will grow into strong plants, blossoming forth into lives of faith and devotion. It is true, we cannot give this to our children as an inheritance, but by word and example we can set an atmosphere in which such qualities can develop.

In this generation, in which there is much aimless living, we would be remiss if we did not consciously attempt to give our children well-rooted lives. This will require that we deal with them in a loving and accepting way. Especially in the earlier years, a child must know that he is loved and accepted by his parents.

PRIDE INSTEAD OF LOVE

Often parents will substitute admiration for love. Their own pride is boosted when a child is good-looking, when he does well in school, or when he has some artistic abilities. We should not wait for the good report card or the witty remark to praise the youngster and to show that we love him. Also, when he is not doing too well, there is need for loving acceptance. There are special times in a child's life when he has great need to know that his parents will not reject him.

But we must also try to give our children wings. In time they must learn to fly away from the parental nest to take on life's responsibilities, and to be able to face life's frustrations and battles. A child can also become too dependent.

OVER-DEPENDENCY

Parents sometimes encourage a spirit of over-dependency. This is covered up with neat little phrases such as, "We have always been a close-knit and loving family"; or, "I want to help my children as long as I can." A child is the most dependent of all creatures and remains dependent on his parents for a longer period of time than any animal. We tend to stretch out this dependency more and more.

But dependency is not only a matter of providing for children financially, or giving bed and board; the real danger is in a deep emotional dependency. Sometimes parents have an emotional need to keep their children dependent upon them.

Teaching our children to have wings begins early in life. The preschool child must already learn to make his little decisions, and then as he grows older he must learn to make greater decisions. No person can ever function as a mature individual unless he has learned to make choices and carry them through.

Overly dependent persons will never really feel secure. They always will want someone else to hold their hand and to give them support. Moving on the road to maturity requires breaking the dependency and developing strong wings to leave the cosy nest.

LEARNING TO FLY

If we have planted the roots well, we need not be afraid when children develop wings. To be sure, they will make mistakes; but we all make them. It is not so serious if they fail at times, but it is important that they know how to grow from each mistake and failure.

When we have planted spiritual roots in our training in the home, the school, and the church, we should be ready to let our children try their wings. This leads also to spiritual maturity and develops spiritual leaders for tomorrow. For a life deeply rooted in God will also develop the wings of faith that enable a person to soar heavenward.

23. Idealization

The trust of a little child is a beautiful thing. Jesus had this in mind when He told us that we must become like little children to enter into the kingdom.

There is an age in the life of a child when he feels that his father and mother are the last word of authority on any subject. If you listen to a dispute between youngsters you will soon hear them say, "My father says so, and he knows," or "My mother told me so." It makes very little difference to them whether the father of the other boy happens to be a world authority on a subject. Their parents know best.

It gives a child a sense of security to be able to have faith in his parents. In himself he is insecure, but when he can be fortified by the stronghold he sees in his parents, he feels strong. Shakespeare once wrote about parents: "For to their children they are heaven's lieutenants."

RESPONSIBILITY

This lays a great responsibility upon parents, one that is not as fully acknowledged as it should be. It is important to be truthful and dependable to our children. We should answer our children's questions honestly. If we do not, as the child grows older, one day he is going to find his fortress crashing in on him, and he will feel most insecure.

If children have been brought up on the theory that babies come from the black bag of the doctor, or from the stork, sooner or later they will find out that the parents have not been dependable. This often results in shocking the child's confidence in his parents, and he will no longer go to them for advice and counsel. His citadel has fallen, and he may well build up resentment.

On the other hand, as the children grow older it is important that they learn to break away from this idealization of their parents. This breaking of the parental bond is never easy for a child, and it often seems most difficult for parents. They hate to see their children grow up, and grow away from them.

Parents unconsciously tend to extend the sphere of their influence by keeping their children tied to their apron strings. Some parents make all the decisions for their children. They decide what they shall wear, where they shall go, what career they must seek in life, and even what life partner to choose.

If children do not learn to emancipate themselves from their parents as youngsters, they will have to learn it later on in life. The older a person becomes, the more difficult it is to do this.

DANGERS

Well-meaning parents often make the mistake of even trying to dominate the lives of their children after they have left the home. It is surprising to see how often this plays a large part in the insecurity that people have later on in life.

Naturally, this process of emancipation must be carried on wisely. And, as a rule, in our civilization it takes place gradually. The children find new authorities in teachers. They find ideals in friends and chums. They find heroes whom they idealize such as star athletes or accomplished musicians. They read it in the lives of great men who have lived in the past, or who are still in the arena of life.

We sometimes see pathetic results of this idealization in married life. When a young man is intent on marrying a girl "just like the girl that married dear old dad," there is potential danger. He is bound for disillusionment. He is going to find out that this girl is different. She cannot bake pies like those that mother used to bake; they may be much better. A bride soon learns that her husband does not match the parent ideal she has. Such people will have to learn to break the parental apron string if they are to make a success of their home.

Occasionally we see students, even on a university level who find such idealization in a professor. They will accept the philosophy of a favorite professor uncritically and in toto. It is not unusual to see some students in a seminary even accept the mannerisms of a professor.

Sooner or later they learn that the opinions of the professor do not always stand up. They must learn a reasonable independence of thought. Hero worship, blindly following a leader, is a frail staff on which to lean. It can at best give security for only a little while.

Some find this sense of security in organizations. This explains to a certain extent the strange power of the lodge. Others may find it in political parties, in labor unions or in cultural organizations. At best, these are poor substitutes for the security that was found in the family home.

A HEALTHY IDEALIZATION

There is a healthier, more solid type of idealization which can be found in the realm of the spiritual life. This is a far cry from a teen-age hero worship. It is far more secure than to rest our ideals in human parents, who so frequently fail, or who are suddenly snatched from us.

For here the soul finds rest in a personal relationship with an unfailing God. The heart finds peace in the person of the Savior. In Him we find that which is perfect in contrast to the imperfections within ourselves.

When the simple, childlike trust is transferred to an unchanging God, in whom all the perfections of life are seen in their fullness, we have an idealization both healthy and abiding.

Life without idealization is empty and void. But when the outgoings of the soul are Godward and heavenward, life has a new dimension. This gives the kind of depth that enables us to ride on serenely over the rough spots of life. It will enable us to walk with the confident swinging step of the Christian. This is life at its best.

24. Children Also Have Rights

Those of us who are parents know that there are often conflicts between us and our children. We have a way of looking at life from a different viewpoint than our growing children. Sometimes we find it hard to understand their reactions, and they often find their parents to be quite unexplainable.

We tend to look at life from opposite directions. As we grow older our energies begin to lessen, but the growing generation seems to be endowed with boundless vitality and vigor, and they feel the need of expressing it. We live with a large storehouse of memories, but the youngsters have few memories. We have often been disillusioned in life, but they have untold optimism for the future.

Children fail to see the importance of going to bed at a certain hour by the clock. They cannot understand why parents should insist upon many of the routine factors of everyday living. They resist the regulations that form an essential part of every family. These contradictions, and many more like them, must be resolved in the home where the generations meet.

In solving these conflicts we must recognize that children have rights as well as do the parents. If we are to achieve a measure of satisfaction and harmony in family life, if the home is to reach its highest purpose, children and parents must respect each others' rights.

PAUL'S INSTRUCTIONS

Even though Paul was not a family man, he writes about the problems of the home with a great deal of insight. To the children in Ephesus, and thus to all Christian children, he writes, "Children, obey your parents." This is a direct command, based upon the specific commandment of God. But then Paul continues to write, "Ye fathers, provoke not your children unto wrath." So with one hand he puts the children in their place, and with the other hand he puts the parents in their place. He shows that the conflict between the generations is a matter for which we are jointly responsible.

As parents we often seize upon the first statement. We assume that parental authority gives us the right to demand obedience, regardless of the reasonableness of our demands. The result is a strongly authoritarian system of government in the family. The will of the parents is law.

When this system is strongly enforced it can prove dangerous. When a child is young, it is impossible to explain the reasons for a parental command. But as children develop and grow it is important for them to see that there are good reasons for the discipline of the home. It may often be easier just to give a command and to compel obedience to it, rather than to give good grounds for it.

But the unreasoned command often leads to rebellion, and many young people have been provoked by parents to this kind of disobedience. But even if it does not lead to a spirit of rebellion, it has the danger that it will lead to a flacid kind of obedience in which a young person will obey rather than to raise a fuss. When this is constantly repeated there is a danger that such a young person will never learn to stand on his own feet, and he will not learn to make his own decisions in life. This is creating over-dependency.

It is also questionable whether an unreasoned command is really successful. You can insist upon it that your daughter of high school age goes to her room to study, but it is quite another thing really to make her actually exercise her brains in study. It requires a good deal more than coercion to instil a desire to learn.

Paul presents the other side of the picture when he tells parents that they are not to provoke their children to wrath. This is equally strong as the previous command. It shows that children also have their rights. Parents are also under higher laws and demands, for when they ask for the obedience of their children they must square these commands with the laws of God and the spirit of Christ.

PURPOSE OF PARENTHOOD

What is the purpose of parenthood? What are we striving to attain in our families? The parental demand for obedience is not to be considered as an end in itself, but it is a means to a higher goal. We are called upon to train our children so that they can ultimately become independent, thinking persons, able to face life and its battles. This must be our goal from infancy.

Moses used the picture of the parent eagle that pushed the little fledglings over the edge of the cliff so that they might learn to use their own wings in flight. We, too, must teach our children to face life, to stand on their own feet. We may feel flattered when, even in adulthood our children are dependent on us, but then we have not done a commendable task of training them. If they cling too long to mother's apron strings, we have created a situation that is fraught with many dangers of an emotional nature. In fact, we may be nurturing a neurotic.

IN THE ADMONITION OF THE LORD

Scripture tells us to nurture our children "in the admonition of the Lord." This brings a common loyalty for parents and children alike. Then parental authority is not one of fear, but one that is sanctified by a mutual love for the Savior of men.

All of life, our daily tasks, our major choices, our nobler endeavors, all must be inspired by a loyalty to the Christ. This will cement a strong relationship between parents and children, one that is not born of fear and coercion but of love.

In this way, parents must reconcile their demands for the obedience of their children to their own obedience to the Christ. Children must be taught to accept parental authority as an evidence of their Christian concern for those whom they love. Then the family becomes a place where the generations meet; but they meet at the feet of Jesus.

TEEN-AGERS IN THE HOME

Remember now thy Creator in the days of thy youth
while the evil days come not
nor the years draw nigh
when thou shalt say, I have no pleasure in them.
Rejoice, O young man, in thy youth,
and let thy heart cheer thee in the days of thy youth
and walk in the ways of thy heart
and in the sight of thine eyes;
But know thou, that for all these things God will bring thee into judgment.

King Solomon – Ecclesiastes

25. The Two Worlds of the Teen-ager

It hardly seems possible to expect to say anything new about the teen-agers of today. Many articles and books have been written; parents and teachers and pastors have frequently discussed this wonderful and perplexing period of adolescence. This has gone on for many centuries, for even the Greeks and the Romans had their say about them. In almost every age there have been those who felt that the new generation was "going to the dogs."

Who can really understand them? One generation always finds it hard to understand the generation preceding and the one following. Even the teen-agers find it hard to understand themselves. In writing on this subject I would not like to pose as an authority. But I would like to share a special concern which has been brought about by recent developments in mental hospitals.

INCREASED HOSPITALIZATION OF ADOLESCENTS

In the last twenty years there has been a constant increase in the number of young people who must be admitted to mental hospitals because of mental breakdowns. This is a national trend. Recent figures show that in the last five years there has been a marked increase to such an extent that one of our Michigan hospitals is building a special building for this purpose.

A recent survey entitled, "Children Hospitalized for Mental Illness," clearly indicated that there is a large increase in admissions of those who are below seventeen years of age. This does not include the mentally retarded who are admitted to state training schools, but only those afflicted with various forms of mental illnesses.

In the four year period between 1931 and 1935 only eighty-three children were admitted. Between 1946 - 1950 the number admitted was two hundred and sixty-four. And of those below seventeen years eight hundred and fifty-one were admitted in four hospitals in Michigan during the years 1956 - 1960. Most of these were between ten and seventeen.

CONTRIBUTING FACTORS

Many reasons are offered for this trend of increased breakdowns in the teen-age years. The demoralization of family life in our country is undoubtedly a factor in our State Hospitals. Statistics showed that over 50 per cent of these children came from broken homes.

A factor that should be considered is that today there are more specialists and more clinics for children so that mental illness is often recognized in its earlier stages. There is also a greater understanding among people about mental disturbances, and many realize that help can be given to those who are afflicted with mental difficulties.

But the fact still remains that a larger number of teen-agers are breaking under the strain of modern living. It is for this reason that I make bold to write about the subject of the mental health of our young people, for it is one of the basic problems that all must face. It is also true that in this area "an ounce of prevention is worth a pound of cure."

A PERIOD OF TRANSITION

Dr. Gordon Allport, a noted psychologist, describes the teen-agers in the following words, "The adolescent is required to live as gracefully as he can in two worlds, the lingering world of childhood and the opening world of adulthood. He is seldom sure of which of these two areas he occupies at a given time."

In a sense these young people are still children. They still have some of the feelings of dependency of childhood. And yet, they have a strong desire to be independent. They need their parents, and yet they desire to break the ties of parental controls.

This is the age in which the tie must be broken. This is sometimes harder for the parents than for the young people, for a child often satisfies certain emotional needs in the parents themselves. It is hard also for the child, for a child is the most dependent of all the creatures. Most young animals can shift for themselves after a few weeks, but a child remains dependent for a number of years.

As the youth grows older he begins to reject his own childishness. He says to himself, and sometimes to his parents, "I am no longer a child, I am a man or a woman." And then again there are times when he needs his parents so desperately; not just for his weekly allowance, but he needs them emotionally. He must know that he is being accepted by them.

To bridge this difficult period of transition gracefully we must remember that the teen-agers live in two worlds, the receding world of childhood and the fast approaching world of adulthood. And as he moves through this segment of the stream of life, he is preparing for the years that lie ahead. For each stage in the developing life is a stepping-stone to the next.

In our civilization the person makes the three greatest choices of his life during these adolescent years. He chooses his life's vocation, he usually chooses his life's mate, and he makes his great spiritual commitment.

So, in a far higher sense he must learn to live in two worlds. While he faces the physical, earthly, material world, he also must live in the spiritual, religious and eternal world. We build our schools, or homes and our churches to help them towards that two-fold citizenship. This is also the faith that helps to build good mental health.

26. The Teen-age Conflict

In a previous chapter we noted that the teen-ager lives in two worlds, the lingering world of childhood and the opening world of adulthood. This would imply that the adolescent years are years of conflict. The pathway that leads from dependence to independence is filled with many hazards. The transition must be made in all areas of life.

INTELLECTUAL CONFLICT

There is possibly no age in which we know more, or think we know more, than in the teen-age years. Many issues that seem to be complex to adults are simple and easy to solve for the adolescent. When we were high school seniors we were ready to make pronouncements about world issues which we would hardly dare to make today. Articles in high school and college publications give eloquent evidence of this fact.

The fact is that during the years from ten to twenty we all gather our greatest storehouse of ideas and facts. Our teen-agers today obtain a great deal of general information and knowledge of many subjects. But they still lack the ripening experience, for they have not had time or occasion to season their knowledge with the wisdom that is gained by actual face-to-face contact with life.

In this sense they have moved from the days of childhood, but still lack the experiential knowledge of adulthood. These are facts that parents and leaders must accept. Their fertile minds and agile brains must be appreciated, and their opinions should be considered. Ridicule and sarcasm does not answer them. There are many stories that place the college trained youth alongside of a poorly educated farmer who is richly endowed with common sense. Usually the college youth must give in to the rural sage, at least, so the story goes.

There is need for an acceptance of the intellectual abilities of youth, but parents and youth leaders must often temper this with wisdom gained in the school of experience. Careful guidance is of the utmost importance.

ADOLESCENT REBELLION

Much of the rebellion of modern youth is not so much against authority, as against their own feelings of childish inadequacy. Parents will say to a boy of sixteen, "You're acting like a child," as though this would be something of which to be ashamed. Surely, he is acting like a child in many ways; that is what you expect of the adolescent, for he is still partly in the world of childhood. He is not quite ready to accept the world of adulthood.

There is often rebellion both against childhood and adulthood. He does not want to be a child anymore, and he is not ready to be an adult. This is part of the conflict of youth, and it is filled with many dangers. He requires a great deal of understanding and guidance during these years of transition.

AN EMOTIONAL CONFLICT

I think we readily forget that these years are often lonely. David Riesman makes this very clear in his book *The Lonely Crowd*. Possibly this is one of the reasons that they feel they must surround themselves with loud and lively music. They also have a strong need for acceptance and friendship by others of their crowd. Maybe this also explains the long telephone conversations that can be rather upsetting to the family routine. They are a lonely crowd.

Basically the adolescent is emotional. The din and noise of high school basketball games can be most annoying to the adults present. But I have had opportunity to see the same young people let their tears flow freely at the funeral of a classmate. They do not want to be emotional, for this is childish, but they have not attained to an adult control of their feelings.

This is often forgotten because of the fact that they can wear a rather hard shell. But when we deal with them more intimately we soon find that they have their anxieties and fears, the times of elation and of depression; and they need opportunity to express their feelings and to be accepted for what they are. This is also one of the wholesome and beautiful aspects of youth. When teen-agers have gotten themselves into trouble it is always a good sign when they can reveal their anxieties. It is part of the conflict of youth.

This conflict is evident also in the developing procreative processes of life. There is within them the gradually developing man and woman, and yet in our culture they are not yet ready to accept the responsibilities of family life.

This can lead to serious problems, especially in an age in which the moral standards of our society are sinking, and when self-expression is being encouraged. Things that were mentioned rather secretly a generation ago, are now openly and blatantly displayed in magazines or on TV.

CONFLICTS OF IDEALS

I feel that as adults we have spent far too much time bemoaning the state of young people, and we have done far too little to try to understand them. It is true that as parents we live in one world; we have passed from the state of childhood, through the transition period, to that of adulthood. (At least, we should have reached that point, both intellectually and emotionally.)

I do not feel that we should generalize when we speak about the youth of today and say that they are worse than in previous generations. There are some who may be worse, but there are others who may rise to greater heights both morally and spiritually. In our present age, with better means of communication, we are in a position to observe teen-agers at their best as well as at their worst.

But we can little expect the adolescent children in our family to rise to greater heights than their parents. When we set lofty spiritual ideals for ourselves, build our homes and our lives on lofty Christian principles, I feel confident that our young people will have similar ideals. The teen-age years can be the most wonderful and the most influential years of our life. They are years of conflict; but with the prayerful guidance of understanding parents, and the undergirding grace of God, our youth will move from the conflicts to victories, conquests that shall be evident in sturdy Christian characters and noble Christlike ideals.

27. Coddling or Counseling Our Adolescents

Certain writers have indicated that it is a lot easier to go through the teen-age years in one of the South Sea islands, than in our culture. In a more simple type of civilization there are few choices that have to be made. The choice of a husband or a wife is made by the parents. There is no choice of occupation and the religion is part of tradition.

In our culture it is quite a different story. At every turn of the road there are complex choices that must be made. There are decisions that influence the rest of a person's life that must be made before the twentieth birthday. The teen-ager stands at the fork of the road.

What are we doing to help them in these years of conflict and often indecision? How can we best help them in this era of transition?

CODDLING OUR CHILDREN

There are many parents who have a policy of pampering their youngsters. Naturally, this does not start after the twelfth year, but it has its beginnings in childhood. This is one of the weaknesses of our generation. It means following the line of least resistance and allowing their children to grow up like Topsy. It is feared that any form of restraint will inhibit their little personalities, and that a definite and firm routine of living will cause them harm.

The result of this kind of training has become evident in our age. When a child has not learned to respect authority, or the rights of others, he will often grow up as a teen-ager who rebels against his parents, his teachers, and often against the laws of God and man.

A friend of mine, who manages a good-sized industrial plant mentioned that the results of this kind of training are evident among working men today. Children have not been taught a sense of responsibility in the home; the school has not been able to imprint a feeling for discipline; so the result is that men enter the field of labor with the same lack of respect for authority. They have never learned to take orders, so why should they take orders from anyone now? In industry they can again hide under the protection of labor unions to give them security.

Coddling is not the answer. The undisciplined person has not developed a strong balanced mental health.

THE RULE OF FEAR

There is an opposite extreme that has fully as many dangers. There are some parents who interpret the fifth commandment to mean that they must constantly assert their authority. Children must obey, without questioning, for the word of the parents is absolute law. Frequent trips to the woodshed are needed to keep the children under control. The youngsters learn to obey, but only because of fear.

It would seem that some parents find a grim satisfaction in browbeating their offspring into submission. But such a child does not learn to respect authority, nor does he see the reasonableness of it. He looks forward to the day when he is big enough, and old enough, to throw off that kind of authority. This often leads to a rebellion against all authority.

The rule of fear is not the answer, for fear is not the kind of emotion that brings out the best in a person; in fact, it often brings out the worst. Such an approach does violence to the very personality of the child; he never learns to make decisions for himself; and it can cause damage to the mental health of a person for the rest of his days.

A RELATION OF CONFIDENCE

The adolescent is in a time of transition. We must try to break the feeling of dependency gradually and gracefully. This does not start in the teens, but when the child is young. Even a pre-school child must learn to make certain choices. As he grows older he must learn to make greater choices. Surely, he will make mistakes, but he will learn also from his mistakes, and the parents are there to guide him so that there may be a growing personality.

In all this a child must be able to confide in his parents. There should be a mutual confidential relationship. It happens rather frequently, when we talk with young people, that we will ask them, "Why didn't you talk this over with your parents?" And they will answer, "Oh, I couldn't talk to them about my problems."

Such a statement indicates that there is something lacking in the parent-child relationship, for it shows that they have not learned to talk to each other in confidence. You can't start doing this when a child is twelve, but this must begin early in life.

THEY NEED COUNSELING

Every child needs to have a chance to talk to one or both of his parents alone. He needs a chance to unburden his heart. We all need that, but especially a sensitive person who is going through a period of life that demands many decisions and choices.

If children cannot confide in their parents, they may sooner or later be talking over their problems with a professional counselor, and then often about problems that have grown to such dimensions that they need real help.

I would contend that the adolescents of today need firm, consistent and loving guidance. They need counseling from those who have already walked the slippery pathway of the teen-age years and have reached a measure of maturity in their own lives. Above all, they need the counsel of those who have found spiritual maturity through a living fellowship with the One who still is "the way, the truth and the life."

28. The Power of Example

The argument about heredity versus environment has been carried on for many years. It is often a futile argument, for the line of separation between the two is too fine to be determined. One can hardly deny that the shape of the nose, or the color of the hair, or the fact that a boy looks just like his father is due to the hereditary line.

But it is more difficult to determine accurately the source of such matters as emotional stability and mental qualities. One thing is sure: that behavioral patterns are set by influences exerted on the child, primarily in the home setting. The home, the school and the church all contribute to influence the pattern of living of children and young people, for they are great imitators during these impressionable years.

It is a bit frightening for parents to think of this fact. We are not only responsible for ourselves, but also for our children, and even our children's children. We form but a link in the chain of the generations. We leave our mark, and prayerfully hope that we have not been a weak link in that chain.

THE EMOTIONAL SETTING

Much of the emotional tone of a child is established already in the early years of life. When the atmosphere of the home is loving and accepting, a child will feel loved and wanted, and will develop a sense of security. But there are also insidious ways in which even Christian parents reveal rejection toward their children. When a child is constantly told to be quiet, when he is often punished severely for little things, and when the parents seldom tell the child that they love him and are pleased with him, a child may well feel that he is not accepted.

This emotional tone carries over into the teen-age years, and even into adult life. A child brought up in an atmosphere of tension will often carry along an attitude of hopelessness, or rebellion. When parents show a great deal of suspicion toward others, you can hardly expect that the child will be different. If parents react unfavorably to frustrations, you may also expect that the son or daughter will be a poor loser and find it hard to face competition.

We take good care of the physical needs of our growing children. We see to it that they get their vitamins and shots. But how about the emotional health and their mental well-being?

THE CULTURAL SETTING

We can instill in our children a love for the beautiful if we provide a setting in which this can be nurtured. The contents of our thoughts are going to be colored by the general setting of the home. If the family stresses social niceties, good manners and proper decorum, this will help the developing child to become a lady or a gentleman. This is taught by example. Parents who never say "thank you" and "please" will find it hard to teach their children to perform such social amenities.

A love for beautiful music and the finer arts is also found in homes where such things are encouraged. The influence of such example will carry over into life and can be a joy to a person all his days.

THE MORAL SETTING

There are inconsistencies in our lives. We all have areas of life in which we do not practice what we preach, for none of us is quite as good as his confession. These inconsistencies will be most evident in the home, for it is there that our faults show most clearly. Children and young people are very ready to note these failings in the parents.

If a family lays a great deal of emphasis upon material advancement, getting ahead in the world, what will prevent a young person from becoming even more materialistic than his parents? If we watch things on TV which are not in good taste, or read literature that is not uplifting, what will prevent our young people from doing the same? If the language used in the home is sprinkled with expressions which border on profanity, what will prevent a young man from taking the name of God in vain?

The atmosphere of the home is so extremely important, for it is sure to carry over into the next generation, and possibly also the ones that follow. The power of example is such a tremendous force in molding the lives of the young. We do well to guard most carefully the example we set.

SPIRITUAL SETTING

Paul said, "the things you have heard and seen in me, do." I wonder how many of us would be willing to say that to our children and young people. There are times when we would like to say, "Don't make the same mistakes I made." For in the spiritual lives of our children there is no more powerful and vital force than the power of example.

When voices are heard that speak about the evils of youth, it is well to take stock of what is going on in our homes and family life. Most likely the spirit of youth reflects the spirit of the home, and the behavior of children reveals the behavior of parents.

The Christian faith must express itself also in the general atmosphere of home and family so that it may be a place that is healthy — emotionally, mentally, culturally and spiritually.

29. Constructive Living in Youth

Someone has described youth as the time between the lingering years of childhood and the opening world of adulthood. It is an extremely important age in the life span of all of us, and it is fraught with a good many dangers.

It is rather hard for those of us who are beyond these years to understand modern teen-agers. We are often a bit alarmed at the type of music they seem to enjoy, at the noisy mufflers that seem to be an essential part of their red cars, and the strange fads they take up. It is often asked whether they are much worse than we were when we were their age. That is of course a question each individual must answer for himself.

CHANGING PATTERNS

It is evident that there have been more changes in the mode of living during the last generation than in any previous one. The inventive genius of man has provided us with many new challenges, and in each of them there also lurks a new danger.

One thing is sure, we have emerged from the isolation which still was possible in the twenties and thirties. We have been hurled headlong into the stream of American life. We cannot live apart from the world, for the world has been brought into our homes, and we have been brought into the midst of the world with all its temptations.

I would not say that this is bad in itself. Today we cannot build a fence around ourselves, and fortify ourselves in our private little kingdoms. This brings with it a new and basic requirement for living in the sixties. We need a much stronger emphasis on a positive approach to life. We have tried too long to live negatively, as though Christianity meant that we had only to avoid certain worldly practices.

Today we need an inner strength of heart and character that enables us to live in the world, and yet not to be of the world. I wonder sometimes whether we have been developing enough strength and power in the inner man.

LIVING SELFISHLY

All of us must guard ourselves against selfish living. Little children are often taught to pray, "Now I lay me down to sleep." This can become a very selfish prayer. It is all "I" and "My." Sometimes children will add "Bless my mother and daddy, and sister and brothers." But there is nothing about the needy, the poor, the destitute and the benighted heathen.

Even little ones should be taught to think of others. For this spills over into adolescence and youth. Many live only for self, and for personal enjoyment. It is for this reason that it is so hard to get young people to give some of their money to the church, or Kingdom causes, at a time when they can best spare some of their cash.

CHRISTIAN SERVICE

But we may thank God that there are young people who live constructively. I think of those who sacrifice a great deal to obtain an education. There are those who have ideals to be teachers, nurses, doctors and ministers.

In the past years I have had opportunity to observe at rather close hand many of these young people. I refer to those who came to our hospital for training in psychiatric nursing.

They are just an average cross section of Christian youth. They are young people who have a noble spirit of adventure.

I have seen many of these young people develop in the few short years they are with us. They grow into strong Christian characters. Many are now bringing up stalwart families of their own. The remarkable thing is that we see many children of former nurses among them.

A YEAR IN HIS SERVICE

The Mennonites, and also the Mormons, require that their young people, who are really dedicated to the faith, give a full year of their lives in some Kingdom enterprise, and that without remuneration. There are two Mennonite mental hospitals which obtain a large percentage of their helpers in this way.

I can think of no finer way to build a Christian life than to spend at least a part of that life in service of our fellowmen.

MANY AVENUES OF SERVICE

There are many ways in which this can be done. A local boys' club undertook the task of mowing and trimming the lawn of an aged couple in the community. The fact that they were of another faith made little difference to the boys. They were lending a helping hand to someone in need.

Another group of high school girls serve as aides at the Children's

Retreat, a hospital-school unit for mentally retarded children. Many others are volunteers in hospitals and children's homes. You may have other projects in your community. They deserve encouragement, for they lead to constructive living on the part of our youth.

Our strongest defense over against the world of today is to develop in our children and young people the inner strength of character that will enable them to move forward into the arena of life, not just to ward off the evils of the age, but constructively to make an impression upon the world.

Our strength is not in our isolation, but in the positive principles that dominate our lives. Our Lord condemns the man who hid his talent in the ground, but commended the one who used his talent well. This is constructive living.

30. Channeling the Enthusiasm of Youth

All around the world youth seems to be in ferment. We often read of student groups that stir up riots and take part in the overthrow of existing governments. The Japanese mob that forced the cancellation of the visit of a United States President was composed largely of teen-agers, incited by agitators.

In Cuba and in the South American countries there often are student protest parades. In our own land the young people have done their bit to add to the confusion of racial segregation and desegregation. This is not something new, for the spirit of youth has manifested itself in different ways in different ages.

The enthusiasm of youth has tremendous potentials. It has potentials for great evil when it is channeled in unworthy and destructive directions. But it has great potentials also for good when it can be channeled into worthwhile and constructive causes.

J. Edgar Hoover, director of the FBI, reports that "the successful exploitation and manipulation of youth and student groups throughout the world is a major challenge which the free world forces must meet and defeat. The vigor and vitality of such groups constitutes an explosive force of tremendous potentials. Channeled into proper outlets, this force can accomplish immeasurable good for a peace-loving world. Manipulated into destructive channels this force can create chaos."

A NEGATIVE APPROACH

To sit back and criticize our youth and its behavior in a negative way has caused more harm than good. Thundering against the evils of juvenile delinquency from the pulpit, or through the press, has never helped the cause very much.

It is rather common that a negative approach is taken. In a good many homes, parents have told their children in no uncertain terms what they may not do, but have failed to provide a constructive program of living. It is not at all unusual for a child in such a home to ask in despair, "Well, what may I do?" This has contributed to the rebellion prevalent in modern youth.

There has been a good deal of this negativism also in the church. We have been inclined to tell people what they may not do, rather than present the great positives of the Christian life. Ministers can readily fall into this error in preaching, and there are many people who find satisfaction in a strongly negative sermon. These are factors that have special dangers in the teen-age years.

During these critical years in a person's life the procreative drives become strong. But these young people are still not able to take up the responsibility of a family. There is need for a healthy and normal inter-relationship between the sexes. If these are not provided, such basic urges can get out of hand. You cannot deny the existence of these inner drives in healthy young people, nor can you submerge them by negatives. But we have not always provided the normal and healthy outlets that young men and women need. I am inclined to believe that this is one of the causes of the large number of forced marriages.

We have had a lot of negativism in recent years. Many of the discussions and arguments have had a strong negative tone. If we would spend as much time building a strong constructive and positive program, we would be much better off. Our strongest defense against the world and its evils is an aggressive battle for the promotion of the cause of Christ. This is true also for our youth.

CHANNELS OF BLESSINGS

Our most vital influence upon our young people will be one that channels the enthusiasm and vitality of youth into constructive programs of Christian living, and into advancement of the Kingdom of Christ. Just to meet in a young men's society, or a girls' club for Bible study and discussion is not enough. The strength of these organizations will be felt only in the measure in which they stir into healthful and spiritual activity. For, youth is a bundle of opportunities; let us beware that we do not lose these possibilities for the King of kings.

Life is a blessing only when it serves as a channel. When the blessings of the Christian faith are ours, we may not just sit back and soak them in like a sponge, but we must allow them to flow through us to others. The man with the one talent was not cast into outer darkness because he wasted his talent in riotous living; he merely hid it in a napkin. The five foolish girls were not shut out of the marriage feast because they hated the bridegroom, but they lacked oil in their lamps.

The real blessing of the Christian life is experienced fully, only when we become channels of blessing. This too will be the greatest blessing for those who live in the thrilling enthusiasm of the teen-age years.

31. The High School Dropout

Since more than one million young people drop out of high school each year, a concerted effort to keep them in school is in progress. Recently the news media have given much attention to this situation.

Actually, this is not a new problem. In fact, the percentage of dropouts has been decreasing. In 1932, two out of three students dropped out of high school. Today the figure is one out of three. It is an encouraging sign that people are becoming more alert to the problem, for many of the young people who make a poor adjustment to life, or who get themselves into trouble, are in this class. A large percentage of the unemployed today are those with less than twelve years of education.

VARIOUS CAUSES

Various reasons have been given for this situation. The National Education Association has ascribed a great deal of it to the fact that the dropout has not learned to read well. Others have felt that the great stress placed on academic excellence has discouraged many young people. They feel that greater emphasis should be placed on programs that permit greater learning satisfaction by giving more vocational training, so that these young people will be better prepared to enter today's labor market.

In many cases it is also a cultural and family problem. In the homes where there is little emphasis on the need for an education and parents do not encourage their youngsters in the need for learning, there is little motivation on the part of the young person to seek further education. Some parents are eager to have their children get to work so they can add to the family income, or, at least, reduce the family expenses. But, as a rule, the young person who is not interested in education is also unwanted in industry.

This problem becomes a serious one, due to the fact that many jobs require special training, training that can be given only to a person with a high-school diploma. Many jobs that were considered unskilled a few years ago have been taken over by computers and automatic machines. This has eliminated the unskilled and untrained worker.

I am sure we have all met young people who have been disillusioned when they enter some sphere of work. They now say, "I only wish I had at least finished high school." Too many doors are closed to them because they contain the sign, "Only high-school graduates need apply."

ENCOURAGEMENT NEEDED

In many high schools the dropout has received little encouragement to stay in school. More than anything else, the dropout needs someone who will take a personal interest in him. Lack of intelligence is not the major problem, since statistics have shown that 70 percent of dropouts have a better-than-average intelligence quotient. It would seem, then, that it is a lack of motivation, or of interest in learning.

John F. Kennedy said, "The future of any country is irreparably damaged whenever any of its children is not educated to the fullest extent of his capacity." He added that the high figure of dropouts is a "waste" this nation cannot afford.

If this is true in a nation, it must certainly also be true in the church. We need well-trained young people who can serve adequately in the consistory, in school boards, and as Sunday-school teachers. The Christian young person has an added incentive for, if he is to be a leader in the community, an effective witness for his Lord, he needs a training that is above the average.

No, you need not be a high-school graduate to be a Christian. But a Christian young person who is serious about his calling in life will want to be trained so that he can most effectively fill his niche in life.

32. Don't Blame Your Parents

It has often been stated that to have good mental health you should choose your parents wisely. It might be even more ideal if you could also choose your four grandparents, for they also have their influence on you.

There has been much discussion throughout the years about the influence of heredity or environment in emotional and mental disturbances. Elaborate diagrams have been developed around the theories of genes and chromosomes. Some of them are rather impressive. There is no doubt about it that there is more mental disturbance in one family than in others.

Some will deny that this is due to heredity. Others will say that we can inherit a disposition towards certain types of mental and emotional sickness, but that you do not inherit the illness. It is true that we do learn to respond to specific situations in life with the same emotional reactions that our parents used. Patterns of reaction to life's disappointments are learned by imitation.

I do not even plan to try to settle the dispute about the influence of heredity and environment. To me that is an academic question, rather than a practical one.

PARENTAL RESPONSIBILITY

I had the privilege of administering the rites of baptism to a child in one of our churches. When I re-read the questions which the parents are required to answer, I felt anew the great responsibility that rests upon us as parents when we confirm our intention to bring up these children to the best of our ability. This is an even greater task when we acknowledge that they are also God's children.

It is always humbling to see the results of our own failures reflected in the lives of our children. I am sure that many of the emotional problems that people carry with them into adult life have been developed in the days of childhood.

Some parents are seriously lacking in the emotional ability to bring up children. To satisfy their own emotional needs they often are overly-protective, or they may be guilty of rejecting them. Many find it hard to break the bond between themselves and their youngsters and thus develop a spirit of overdependency in them.

Most of us do not train our children in an adequate way to face the disappointments and frustrations of life. None of us ever rears a child in a perfect way, for parents are also human.

PARENTS ALSO HAD PARENTS

But this does not mean that you can blame your parents for everything that goes wrong in your emotional life. Nor does it mean that when a person is well adjusted to mature living we can conclude that he must have had ideal parents. Possibly his parental training was inferior to others who are now poorly adjusted.

When we blame our parents we are forgetting that they also had parents who in turn trained them. So you can move back up the ancestral tree, and if you shake it hard enough, you may be able to find someone upon whom you can pin the blame. Many factors go into the development of a human being; it is a complex matter, and there is not one, but there are many things that may account for the emotional development of each of us.

PERSONAL RESPONSIBILITY

Within each of us there is the potential to rise above the environmental and hereditary level, but there is also the danger that we fall below this line. If Abraham Lincoln had remained in the family tradition he would have been one of the rustic railsplitters of his home community. But there was something in his personality that led him to break with the family tradition and to become one of our greatest presidents.

There is a responsible inner element in each one of us. It is that which makes you a person with qualities that differ from any other person. This also makes you accountable for what you are in your thoughts, actions and emotional attitudes. It is a flimsy excuse for a man with a violent temper to say, "Yes, my dad used to get awfully angry too." It is a sad commentary when a person with a severe emotional instability tells us that she came by it honestly, because her mother had the same problem.

Parents should help their sons and daughters to think and act for themselves, and to develop a healthy detached relationship to them. But those same sons and daughters cannot go through life blaming their parents for their emotional immaturity. It would mean that they refuse to take personal responsibility for what they are. They would still be slaves to the family line.

HANDICAPS CAN BECOME ASSETS

Psychiatrists and counselors will often try to have a person with problems trace the origin of these problems to their early and formative days. This is not done to blame the parents, but to lead the person to a new feeling of a more detached and responsible attitude towards themselves.

If your childhood home has not been a happy one, it can then serve as an incentive to make your own home a place where your children can find satisfaction and acceptance. If your father drank to excess, you are in a wonderful position to know the evils of such a life, and to make your own life a better example for your children.

The danger we all face is that of carrying our family traditions on into the following generations. If these are good traditions, this is a wonderful thing. But if the spirit of the family has been one of emotional, mental and spiritual instability, be sure to break it off so that you will not pass it on to the generations to follow.

Each person stands as a responsible link in the chain of life. As you stand in the presence of the Giver of Life you can't blame your parents for what you are. You can't blame your environment. For God has placed in each one of us, who has a sound mind, the potential to live constructively and maturely. But to do this, we must avail ourselves of the marvelous resources that He offers us. "But we have this treasure in earthen vessels, that the exceeding greatness of the power may be of God, and not from ourselves."

It is a wonderful thing that Christ counts each of us to be a responsible person, for this makes life interesting and worth living.

33. Do You Want to Grow Up?

There are a number of people who never reach emotional and mental maturity because they do not want to grow up. They would never admit this, for this would sound rather infantile, but their actions and reactions reveal that inwardly, unconsciously, they do not desire to be reasonably mature.

In our attempts to develop inner controls in children and young people, we proceed on the assumption that everyone really wants to grow up. We appeal to a teen-ager with the statement, "You are acting like a child." We try to put them to shame, but, possibly, this is just what this young person wants. He wants to be a child.

The act of growing up always implies change and development. This will mean losing some of the supports that we had when we were children. It will mean that we have to go on our own. A little child that is learning to walk finds it hard to let go of his parent's hand, for he is afraid that he will fall when he loses that grip. It is usually an anxious moment when he takes his first step alone, and the step is usually a faltering one.

INDECISIVENESS

In this same way some people have a hard time making a decision. To choose to do something different always means that we have to relinquish something in which we felt safe. Launching out into something new requires a certain amount of courage and confidence.

Others find it hard to change to anything new or different. They feel safe as long as they can cling to the old, but anxious as soon as there is something new. I have seen a number of people who broke down emotionally when they moved from one house to another. The new house was most likely much nicer, much more comfortable than the old, but they could not endure the change.

Some find this also when they take on a new position in their work. They were well acquainted with the routine of their old job, but the new work is strange; they walk in areas where they feel insecure and anxious. It is for this reason that there is so much tension and job insecurity in these changing times. Many have a hard time adapting to the changes of modern inventiveness.

Many of these insecure people do not want to grow up. They

are more comfortable, more secure in the protected atmosphere of their childish attitudes. They want to remain dependent, for this helps them to run away from realities, and it is often easier for them to do this than to face reality squarely.

"Why bother about changing; the old things are good enough" is the attitude of many also within the church. The things that were good enough for father and mother, are supposedly good enough for us today. This clinging to tradition, merely because it is safer and easier, is a poor approach to life. It is not a life built on principle and conviction, but one built on expediency.

THE FEAR OF CHANGE

With the changing times and trends in our generation, we may well have to make changes to adapt ourselves. The old is not always the best, nor is the new always the best. But inflexibility, the fear of change, is dangerous in an age such as ours.

Sometimes rigidity of thought patterns is considered to be a mark of a strong person. It may be, but it may also be the mark of a man who does not dare to look at both sides of the issue. He may be afraid that he will have to change some of his ideas. This is a mark of immaturity.

We may never sacrifice our convictions, we may not yield our principles, but we may have to change our insights so that we can accomplish the great things of life. Only those who dared to venture out in faith have accomplished great things.

The complacent attitude of many Christians today is a mark of both emotional and spiritual immaturity. We are too easily satisfied because we are afraid to venture into anything new and different. The great men of Scripture, the great men of history and science, were the ones who dared to stand out from the crowd and move ahead. This should also mark the Christian man in an age such as ours.

Paul was no weakling; he dared to walk alone. But he had this confidence because he had learned to place his hand in the hand of God. In this spirit he could be "more than a conqueror."

34. Ill-defined Goals

In the past few months it has been my privilege to contact a number of high schools and to talk to the students about their goals and objectives. Naturally, it was my aim to interest them in the field of service related to mental health. It is very encouraging to note that a number of our young people are deeply interested in fields of service.

It is most interesting to listen to some of the questions that arise in their energetic and idealistic minds. An attractive young lady will ask, "How long must I go to school to become a social worker?" A bright young man asks about the requirements for becoming a psychiatrist or psychologist. Often, when the facts are made known, the student will indicate such a program is a bit too ambitious for one who is already tired of school in his senior year of high school.

These young people do have goals and aspirations, but their goals are often ill-defined. They know what they would like to take up in life, but they find that the price of reaching the goal is a bit too high. They have goals, but they are not too realistic.

A RESTLESS SPIRIT

Much of the prevailing restlessness and tension in our age is born out of a lack of adequate purpose in life. There are many in college who have not definitely settled the choice of life's vocation. Some have already graduated and still have no well-defined goals for living. This can be seen in the restless shifting of many in the arena of life.

One of the goals often acclaimed is the desire to be successful. This is a vague sort of thing. If a person wants to be a financial success, it is a question what he has in mind. Does this mean that he must accumulate $50,000 or $500,000 to be considered successful? If a man seeks success in politics, it is a question whether this means that he wants to be a city alderman or a United States Senator. If a person wants to have success as a teacher, does this mean that he must have a Ph.D. and teach in a university, or is he satisfied to teach mathematics in a junior high school? The search for success is always a relative and ill-defined goal; it is an inadequate ultimate.

The failure to have well-defined goals leads to much frustration and conflict. To find real integration of the resources of the self, we need to have a goal that we feel we can reach. People are told today to "think big." But some people think so big that they can never reach their goals.

BEING REALISTIC

It may be well to encourage Johnny with the thought that someday he may be president of the United States, but it may be far more realistic to set for him the immediate goal of getting a decent mark in his chemistry course. It may be well for a high-school student to say, "I want to be a psychiatrist," but it is far more realistic to have him set as his first goal to get through college, then to seek his M.D. degree, and then he can see whether he has the stamina and the cash to take five more years of training and residency.

We all have to face life in sections that we can handle. Many persons have been lost for the present-day struggle because they are dreaming of future success.

I feel that this attitude contributes to much of the tension among young people today. Every good science student is encouraged to become a nuclear scientist, and every student adept at electronics must become a computer expert. In such a scheme of things there are bound to be frustrations and failures, and a large number become discouraged and tend to give up. For even though a child may have the mental ability to accomplish such goals, he may not be suited for such tasks emotionally.

THE LOFTIEST GOAL

The better answer to all of this is to find a well-defined goal for living. Jesus tells us to "seek first the kingdom of God." This must always be the great goal and purpose of all of us. But then, let the lesser goals find their place in their own time. The earthly goals are often ill-defined, but the spiritual ones remain the same from age to age and, through God's grace, these goals are attainable.

35. Giving Advice

To ask for advice and to give it are natural processes. If your neighbor's daughter has just had the chicken pox and now your child has it, you will most likely ask for advice, or perhaps your neighbor will give the advice whether you ask for it or not. People often give unsolicited advice and find that it is not too well accepted.

Sometimes it is necessary for parents or pastors or teachers to give unsought counsel. This can be most difficult to do. People will also ask for advice and then refuse to accept it because it does not agree with their own opinions.

DIFFICULT AREAS

There are certain circumstances in life in which advice is very difficult to give. One of these is the matter of inter-family relationships. When there is rough sailing on the sea of matrimony, many people need advice, they may even ask for it, but they find it hard to accept. The counselor is in danger of becoming the third party who, in trying to be helpful, finds that both husband and wife turn against him.

It is also most difficult to give counsel to those who are contemplating marriage. When two young people feel that they are in love with each other, even when that love may be on a shaky basis, advice is seldom accepted in good grace. When a young man asks, "Is it wise to marry this girl?" he is often looking for only one answer, "Go ahead, and marry her."

And yet, even in such difficult cases advice should be given. Parents would be sadly remiss if they did not give their counsel, and pastors would be seriously neglectful of their duties if they refused to advise in these critical areas of life.

There are certain fundamentals that should be observed in giving advice. In stating these basic thoughts I would not like to pose as an authority on this subject. I merely give a little advice on this matter of giving advice.

THE ART OF LISTENING

One of the primary requirements for giving counsel is to learn to listen. It is sheer folly to immediately dish out advice without having heard what the person has to say on the matter. Quite often people will suggest a solution to their own problems, if they are allowed to unfold their story.

Most of us are poor listeners and ministers and teachers are no exception. We tend to talk too much and listen too little. Often when talking to people we will notice that while we are talking they are thinking about what they are going to say next.

But listening does not mean that we just sit there and let the other person talk. We must direct their conversation by understanding comments and questions. We must show a friendly spirit and show that we are interested in what they are saying.

Even more important we should note how they feel about the matters they are discussing. Often people do not reveal their real problem in the things they say, but they do reveal themselves in the way they show their feelings.

EMPATHY

As you talk with people try to put yourself in their place. This is more than sympathy, it is empathy. To really advise someone you must take the viewpoint of the other person, and try to move from there to a proper solution of the problem. If you remain an outsider, looking in, you cannot help others very well. You must try to be one with them.

In this spirit you must talk over the matter with them. It is not good to say, "This is the answer, this you must do." Rather come with a suggested solution and say, "What do you think of this possibility?" "Wouldn't this be a good way out of your difficulty?" Or suggest several possibilities and then come to a solution with them.

Giving advice is not a matter of forcing your opinion on some other person. It is important to try to gain their acceptance of a good answer to their problem.

This does not mean using "soft-soap methods." It is giving advice in an understanding way. You come then not with your authority but with your friendly acceptance of the person.

THUS SAITH THE LORD

Most important of all, in giving advice, is to allow the person to see that the advice is not just your own words, but that God has spoken. I know of no more powerful means of convincing people of the rightness or the wrongness of their course of life than to be able to substantiate your words with the powerful Word of God.

Too much advice is on a purely human level. If we can lift our counsel out of the "I think" level to the higher plane in which we hear God speak, our advice and counsel will be far more effective. True counseling means that we carry on a conversation with a person, but as we speak to them, we hope that God will carry on His great conversation with the soul. And we pray that the soul will then respond to God, will answer Him and obey His word. And when He speaks, who then would dare to resist Him?

36. A Generation of "Beatniks"

In 1961 the PTA of our local high school adopted and distributed a code of ethics for teen-agers in our Christian community. Guidelines for conduct were developed on such matters as when young people should return home after a date, the kind of clothing that should be worn, and the use of automobiles. It was felt that if there were greater uniformity in these matters, parents would find it easier to enforce certain standards of behavior.

There was a time when the enforcement of codes of ethics was left largely to the home. Parents tried to guide the members of the family by means of the needed discipline. The teachers in the school added their influence to that of the home, and the church stressed the same basic concepts of behavior. When a community-wide code must be adopted, it implies that the home has not been fulfilling its true function.

PARENTAL NEGLECT

It is quite evident that many parents have failed in setting proper standards for their children. It has become customary to take a more permissive attitude in the matter of child training. Books of child psychology have stressed that children should not be inhibited, for this might frustrate their natural development. Parents are urged to be a "pal" to their youngsters.

As a result, parents have developed a vague fear that discipline could frustrate the child and create tendencies that could undermine his mental health. Such restraints might prevent the full development of personality, and children would grow up to be neurotics. Consequently, children are not given disciplinary guidance during their formative years.

We are reaping the results of this approach in our generation. In the American world there are many undisciplined children and teen-agers and, as a result, also many undisciplined adults. Leaders in the industrial world complain that there are a number of workers who enter the labor market who have never learned any self-discipline, and hence do not take kindly to any form of authority.

MODERN LITERATURE

The approach toward what is right and what is wrong has also changed. This is evident in the "best sellers" that are on the literary market. The hero, in the modern novel is often a person who is shiftless and lacks moral standards. Homosexuals, drug addicts, perverts and alcoholics, dope pushers and even molesters of children receive wide acclaim in literary circles.

The modern "beatniks" also enjoy flaunting the conventional codes of living. Their form of dress, their type of entertainment, their abhorrence of the use of soap and water, their poetry and songs all give free expression to their rebellion against restraints of society and religion. In their smoke-filled coffee houses they like to think of themselves as liberated people. Even their language requires a new dictionary.

All this is but part of the rebellion that is evident in the rise in delinquency, crime, and the rejection of moral standards.

A REBELLIOUS SPIRIT

The fact that a PTA felt it necessary to make use of a code is an indication that the "beatnik" spirit is also found in the Christian community. We are not escaping the contamination of the age.

To be sure, we need a moral code, a guide for behavior, but it should not have to be one that is written by a PTA. Nor should it be rules adopted by a synod. As Christians, our code of ethics should be written on our own hearts. It must grow out of the Christian principles that lie within. It should not be the command, "Thou shalt," but the inner urging that says, "I will."

Our Lord was ready to oppose the standards and conventions of his day, but in his perfect purity He walked among the children of men and said, "Follow Me." There is little room for the "beatnik" attitude among those who follow in his train.

37. Building Air Castles

Children usually go through a period in life when they live in a world of fantasy. The dolls and toy fire engines they play with become real to them, and they picture themselves as living in the world of adults. Daydreams can sometimes be very real to an impressionable person, and it is normal to find a certain amount of them in our lives, especially when we are younger. We recognize them, however, to be the products of our imagination.

A WORLD OF FANTASY

But when a person drifts into the habit of spending a great deal of time in his wishful thinking, he is developing a real emotional and mental hazard. In adult life the world of fantasy provides an escape from the realities of life that are not too pleasant, and it prevents a person from solving his problems realistically. Instead of facing the unpleasant facts of life, the habitual daydreamer builds air castles and lives in a make-believe world.

A man who works in the shipping department or stock room of a factory may well dream of the day when he will inherit a fortune and be able to be the owner of the company. Such dreams are then only an escape from the monotony of the work he is doing. There are success stories of newsboys who have gradually climbed up the ladder until they were the editors and publishers. But these men did a lot more than just dream.

A girl who feels that she is not too attractive and hence has feelings of inferiority may dream of the handsome young man who will pick her up in his Cadillac convertible. There are stories of lowly household maids who have married millionaires, but this did not take place by living in a world of fantasy.

UNREALISTIC DREAMS

Every person can be a superman or a glamor girl in his air castles. But this does not mean that we are so in the real world in which we are called to live. Even though there may be some whose dreams have come true, there are vast multitudes who have been deeply disillusioned by building castles in the air. Man has the capacity to fool himself by his wishful thinking.

For daydreaming and building air castles is a flight from reality, an escape into a world of make-believe. Every daydream is an unfulfilled wish. It represents a desire that has not been granted. It shows that a person is withdrawing from the competition and struggle of a rough-and-tumble world. It often is the cause that prevents a person from doing his best in his assigned work.

It is good to have dreams for the future, provided we can take positive action to seek their fulfillment. But when these fantasies are far beyond our reach or our capacities, they are only means of escaping from the realities and frustrations of life.

The person whose ambitions far exceed his abilities is going to suffer many bitter frustrations, and these are frustrations of his own making. He has set his goals too high and, as a result, develops tensions that endanger his emotional health. It is important that we all learn to recognize our limitations and learn to live with them. We must make our goals realistic. This is not easy in our age when there are many people who live in comparative luxury. The desire for more of this world's goods is often one that can never be fully satisfied, for the more we have, the more we want.

PERSONAL LIMITATIONS

We have children in the Children's Retreat who are limited to a greater or a lesser degree. We might wish that we would be able to teach one of these youngsters to read and write and take care of himself. But it would be sheer folly to try this; for when impossible goals are held before these children, their frustrations would become well-nigh unbearable.

There are emotional, mental, and physical limitations with which we all must live. No man can be at the top in every field of learning or in every kind of work. The Lord has given each one of us certain talents and abilities. He only requires that we use and develop these to the best of our ability. He does not ask that we overreach ourselves, for He knows the dangers of such actions.

We must learn to limit our desires. This is especially true in the world in which you and I live. Paul tells us that he has learned to be content "in whatever state I am." This contentment is a bit scarce today, even in the lives of many Christians. I am confident that our Lord discourages us from building castles in the air fully as much as building our houses on sinking sand. In fact, the two are very much alike.

KEEPING THE HOME IN BALANCE

Love suffereth long, and is kind;
Love envieth not;
Love vaunteth not itself, is not puffed up;
Doth not behave itself unseemly,
Seeketh not its own,
Is not provoked,
Taketh not account of evil;
Rejoiceth not in unrighteousness
But rejoiceth in the truth.
Beareth all things,
Believeth all things,
Hopeth all things,
Endureth all things.
Love never faileth.

Paul — I Corinthians 13

38. Twentieth Century Idolatries

The philosopher, John Stuart Mills, once said that if he would reach all that he longed for, if all his aspirations in life were fulfilled, he would feel that life was no longer worth living.

The trouble with people who feel that they can achieve their aspirations is that their goal or ultimate is defective. They have set up ideals for themselves that are inadequate to satisfy the longings of the soul.

There are many people who have such inadequate ultimates. This is merely another way of saying that they are idolaters, for they worship something that is less than God.

I am convinced that even within the Christian church there are those who worship idols, who have gods of their own making upon which they have set their devotion and their love. One of these idols is material wealth. I am not thinking only of the money that is needed to pay the gas bill or to make payments on the mortgage, but the desire for wealth, for riches.

There is something inviting about having riches. They unlock doors for luxurious living, they give a sense of prestige and status that can be found in no other way. They have a strange power over the human spirit. A day's visit in Las Vegas, and a view of the people at the gambling tables, will show how the lure of riches inflames the imagination and goads men to greed.

Money can be like a god – a false god – that entices the hearts of men. It can have a god-like control over the soul. In many hearts and homes it occupies the throne.

But money is a defective ultimate. Even the things that money can buy will in time weary us. Many have the idea that these things will give a sense of security and well-being. Wealth makes a man feel independent and self-sufficient. Patients who come to the hospital will often say, "I haven't a thing to worry about, because we do have adequate means."

The possession of wealth, or the lack of it, can change a person's life radically. In this world a man may be a genius and have great talents and noble traits of character, but if he does not have money in his pocket he is counted as a failure. A man may be lacking in intelligence and character, but if he is rich, others will bow before him and consider him a success.

We have all seen changes take place in people when they gained wealth. Men who were faithful leaders in the church, often consistory members, have refused to take an active part in such work when they became rich. Others have felt the need of changing to a church that was more in their social and financial class.

AN INADEQUATE ULTIMATE

The god of our age is overlaid with gold. But actually this god is an illusion – an inadequate ultimate. It does not provide peace of mind and heart. For wealth can never buy love, nor can it buy emotional and mental health. Men may worship at its shrine, but such worship will only leave them empty and barren.

Over dependence upon an inadequate ultimate leads to a sense of frustration and insecurity. The worship of money is a common cause for anxiety. Statistics have amply shown that more people worry more about material goods than about any other single thing. This is true not only of those who have wealth, but even more so of those who do not possess it. For in the lives of those who are poor there is often a strong drive for wealth.

Poverty is no virtue, neither is wealth; all depends on our attitude toward the material world. Money, or the love of it, can hide the face of God. But we can also use money as a means to serve and honor. It is not how much you have, but what you are that counts. Our Lord said, "A man's life consisteth not in the abundance of the things which he possesseth."

39. In Search of Pleasure

Speakers and writers often describe our time as a "pleasure-mad age." This is a good description of the present generation. But it is well to remember that the "pleasure-pain" principle has governed the lives of people of all time. It is instinctive in us, as also in the animal world, to seek the things that give pleasure and to avoid the things that give pain.

But often pleasure becomes a goal in itself; for some people it seems to be the highest ideal of life. Then the search for pleasure becomes idolatry.

COMPARTMENTALIZATION

There is also a growing tendency to divide life into various categories. A line of distinction is drawn between work and pleasure as though they were opposites. Students, when they come to the end of a term, having finished the examinations, will say, "Now we can have some fun."

Men and women go about their work in the same spirit. They must work for a living a certain number of hours per day, but when it is finished they find time for pleasure. This dualistic view of life is dangerous, for it views only relaxation as a time of pleasure.

There is a vast army of people who are dedicated today to the entertainment industry. They work to provide pleasure for the masses. Our society is directed to the creation of mass pleasure, rather than individual pleasure. The aim is to satisfy the thirst for entertainment on a mass scale. It is geared as a rule to the lowest common denominator.

LIMITS OF PLEASURE

The difficulty with pleasure is that it demands an ever greater stimulus to really give satisfaction to a person. It has this strange quality about it that doubling the time of a given pleasure does not give a person twice as much enjoyment. A trip of five hundred miles is not going to give a person more pleasure than one of fifty. A wealthy man may spend twice as much for his vacation as a man with less means, but this would not assure him to have twice the pleasure of the other.

You cannot increase pleasure by merely doubling it. It demands new interests, new means of entertainment, and new sources of amusement. As a result, it tends to leave us with an empty and discontented feeling. It does not really satisfy the deeper centers of life. This possibly explains some of the tragic dissatisfaction with life that is found in the lives of many today.

Many of the leaders in the entertainment field present a tragic picture. Large numbers of actors and actresses need the help of psychiatrists, and too many of them either attempt to commit suicide, or actually do so. These people have been well described as the priests and the priestesses of the idols of pleasure, for they officiate at the temples where many worship the idol of pleasure.

NOT A GOAL IN ITSELF

Actually, pleasure has this strange quality that, when you seek it as a goal in itself, you will not find it. To possess it, one must not seek it directly but rather seek it through something else. It does not cause itself, but it is caused by the possession of some good, or the attainment of some worth-while goal.

We should learn again the art of finding individual enjoyment rather than being part of the mass of people who must be entertained. The enjoyment of reading a good book, listening to great music or viewing the grandeur of nature have been swallowed up by the popular entertainers of the day whose only interest is really a financial one. Learn to find your pleasure in the ordinary things of life, in the work you do, in family living, and in your friends.

The world we see in magazines and on TV is actually unreal, it is not the world in which you and I live. For the Christian the world has another dimension. So we find our real pleasure in the blessings of the soul as it looks up to God. These are pleasures that can only be experienced by the Christian.

40. Not Status but Stature

Vance Packard presents a vivid picture of modern life in a book entitled *The Status Seekers* (1959). Some of the observations of this best seller are superficial and lacking in objectivity, but his warning against the growing pursuit of status is timely.

Among our ancestors in Europe there was also a great deal of emphasis on "stand," or class distinction. A person belonged to either the upper, middle, or lower class of society. This depended largely upon financial means, the profession or business one operated, or the work that was done to make a living. These distinctions were then carried on through the generations. In England the social levels were dignified with titles that marked the position on the ladder of social status.

It is a well-known fact that these class distinctions have given rise to many emotional and social problems. Children in the upper class were expected to achieve, often far beyond their individual abilities. When they failed, they were a source of disgrace to the family. This led to much frustration, anxiety, and tension. Daughters would sometimes marry outside of their social class and experience great problems of marital adjustment. Many neuroses and mental disturbances arose in such a setting.

STATUS A CLOAK FOR ANXIETY

In our land there are no aristocratic titles and no class distinctions as evident in many countries. But we are caught up in the fascinating game of obtaining and displaying many status symbols.

This is a land of opportunity. We have the world's highest standard of living, a remarkable wage scale, and a fairly healthy level of employment. Here we can achieve on the basis of our own abilities and capacities, rather than on the basis of our ancestry. Each person has opportunity to climb up the ladder of success.

But the mark of success that we have set for ourselves is measured in terms of material status symbols. A spacious house on the right street, a late model car with an abundance of chrome, fashionable clothing, and a well-planned vacation in summer and winter are all marks of success. They mark the status we have achieved.

There are some real dangers inherent in this passionate pursuit of status. The same dangers that were found under the social structure of Europe are in evidence also today. We often get so caught up and preoccupied with the American symbols of success that we forget the more basic goals of living. There is also the endless cycle of competition that keeps us anxious and tense at all times. For the status symbols change with each decade.

Children in school already form their little cliques. They describe those who are not in their group as being "out of it." Fraternities and sororities in colleges and universities give rise to this same kind of snobbery.

But the pursuit of status indicates a basic insecurity and spiritual discontent. People are not ready to accept themselves for what they are, and they try to cloak their basic anxieties with symbols of luxury. It is little wonder that in some circles even having a psychoanalyst is part of the status symbol.

WHAT'S YOUR STATURE?

To set the pursuit of status as a goal in itself is to pursue an empty and illusive ideal. When social ambition dictates what is best for ourselves and our families, our moral standards are submerged to social standards. This is inadequate.

The true standards of judgment for a man are not what he has, but what he is. It is not his status but his stature that counts. We must value the qualities of personality and character rather than what a man earns or how much he is worth.

Judged by the standards of many today, Jesus would have been a failure and Peter and John would have been "out of it." And yet, the men who have really made life count were those who rose head and shoulders above the rest of men because of their moral and spiritual stature. We could release ourselves from a lot of useless tension if we would give heed to the words of Jesus:

"A man's life consisteth not in the abundance of the things which he possesseth." And of the foolish rich man He said: "So is he that layeth up treasure for himself, and is not rich toward God."

41. Snob Appeal

One of the strongest drives in man is the desire to achieve, to get ahead in this world. The advertising industry is geared to this desire for greater status. People are classified as being in the Chevy or Ford class, or being in the Cadillac class. The appeal is made to "those who want the very best." This has more aptly been described as "snob appeal."

A buyer in a department store told me that people buy clothing not so much because it looks good on them as because it puts them in a certain class. The labels in suits and dresses are an important factor in the search for status.

This is also a real factor in Christian circles. Often patients will use the expression, "The group of our church we run around with." Usually this means the members of the church who are within the same age group, but also in the same financial brackets, who drive the same class of cars, and who live in the same kind of homes. Church members, too, are often far more conscious of status than we like to admit.

A DESIRE TO ACHIEVE

It is true that the desire to achieve in life is not in itself wrong. When it is properly directed, it can be one of the most potent factors in a Christian's life. But when status becomes an end in itself it is not only dangerous; it becomes an idol that we worship.

But there are more status symbols that drive people. It is not only the material things, such as houses, furniture, and a motor boat. It is also evident in people who look for a position of esteem and honor. We want other people to admire us, to respect us, and to look up to us. This again in itself is not wrong. Solomon says, "A good name is rather to be chosen than great riches."

As human beings, we are constituted with a need to have the trust and the esteem of others. The most noble traits of personality are nurtured in an atmosphere of the respect of our fellow men. One of the tragic factors that often accompanies mental illness is the feeling that others do not understand and do not care. Mentally ill persons often lose their sense of self-respect because they feel that others do not respect them.

But honor can also become an idol. Men are often willing to sacrifice their religious principles, their moral scruples, and considerable financial assets to gain the honor and esteem of others. They are willing to be all things to all men, just so that men will admire them.

AN EMPTY SHRINE

But worship of such an idol means that we worship at an empty shrine. Seeking for status and honor is a vain search. A man may achieve a certain status, so that he lives in a certain social and economic class, but he soon meets others who are in a higher class, and so he feels displeased with what he has. If status is his idol, he will find that his search is never ending, never satisfying.

In previous chapters we have traced briefly some of the forms of modern idolatry. Money can be an idol, and many worship mammon. Pleasure may be an idol, and many worship at its shrines. Status and honor may also be idols, and many bow before these false gods.

All idolatry leaves the soul empty and void. It is a search for something that has no lasting satisfaction. For that reason it always undermines the mental and emotional life of a person. Much of the restlessness and insecurity of people today is surely due to this fruitless search for something meaningful, something that satisfies the deeper needs of man. Only when a person is guided by true values does his life gain meaning.

In an atomic world, money, pleasure, and honor are fragile reeds upon which to lean. These symbols cannot endure the blast of one atomic weapon. It is only when we see that we live in a meaningful universe, governed by a living and loving God, that life takes on true meaning. Only when we see God's redemptive purpose in all things can we gain security at such a time as this.

42. Living above the Average

I have before me a questionnaire of evaluation for a young lady who desires to enter another school of nursing. In order to estimate her character and industry I must underline whether she is average, above average or below average. We use this form of recommendation often in life. Sad to say, for many we must underscore the word "average" much too often. Generally we tend to be just average.

The report cards in our schools tell us that a mark of "C" is average. I am convinced that it is not the average of ability but the average of performance. Usually people do not operate at the maximum of their ability, nor at the minimum, but somewhere between the two.

But when we only strive to reach the average the tendency is that it soon leads to the minimum average, rather than the maximum average.

Patients will tell us, "My husband is better than the average, and our home life is better than many others." Actually, this is a miserable standard of judgment. Real love is not interested in mediocrity. Since the general level of home life in our country is rather sad, just an average situation is not enough.

A DANGEROUS ATTITUDE TOWARD LIFE

The danger of limping along under the impetus of the average mind is that it leads to the feeling that work is drudgery. It has to be performed and so the less there is the better for us. Life consists then of doing things that we must do, and little more. It leads us to be slaves to the "oughts" of life rather than to be driven by higher motives born out of noble ideals.

Children have a way of doing this. The girls will say, "If I wash the dishes, must I also dry them?" Boys will ask, "If I mow the front lawn, must I also mow the back lawn?" At school they will also try to get by with the minimum that is required of them.

This is evident also in giving for the church, the kingdom, or community ventures. Giving has become, to a large extent, a matter of requirement. We are encouraged to give the average amount, and we tend to feel that when we have done that we have fulfilled our obligations.

This is a dangerous attitude towards life, and yet it is one into which many of our people have fallen. We are so content to live like the rest of men. Few fall below the level, and few rise above the level. Few people bring out their worst, but few rise to the real level of their ability.

A NEW DIMENSION

It is the result of living too much in the spirit of the "must" in the Christian life and not enough in the realm of "desire." We do what is required of us, and little more. But there is a large realm of the Christian endeavor that rises to far greater heights. We should add a new dimension of living, for when we do only that which is required of us we tend to hide a great deal of our latent ability and talent, and we allow many of our best qualities to remain pent up within us.

We tend to divide life into compartments. Our daily work, our regular church activities and our regular duties in the home are things that must be done. But our hobbies and recreational activities are the things we really like to do. So we tend to do the one in a routine way, while the other receives our enthusiastic interest. I pity the man who spends his days like that and the woman who takes this outlook upon life. The real joy is found when we can put all of life under the area of desire and enthusiastic endeavor.

There are nurses in our hospitals who carry out their orders to the letter; they are efficient in their work, but their attitude shows that their chief reward is found in the pay check at the end of the month. There are others who carry out their work with bouncing enthusiasm, for they love their work. They are always ready to do the little extra things that make a patient feel more at ease. These have taken the drudgery out of their work. They have learned to view their work in the light of One who said, "Inasmuch as ye did it unto . . . these, ye did it unto me."

THE COMMAND OF CHRIST

It is plain that the minimum mind is altogether normal in our time. It is evident that many have not been touched by the command of Christ to be ready to go "the second mile." Here lies the real satisfaction of Christian living. To give that extra dollar reveals the real heart of Christian giving. To perform that extra task, that is beyond the realm of duty, shows the heart beat of Christian service.

It all depends on your attitude. If you are content to be marked "average" you have lost a good deal of life's idealism. For the minimum mind is sluggish and bored, just plodding along in a rut. But to be committed to the maximum is a thrilling thing.

Generally speaking, people do not like those who live above the average anymore than they can condone those who live below the average. John Bunyan was in jail with hardened criminals. Jesus was nailed to the cross hanging between two men who had fallen far below the average.

In the world the ideal is, an honest day's work for an honest wage. In the Kingdom of Christ the ideal is to go beyond the realm of duty. When Jesus lived in this world he was not content to live just within the demands of the law, but He gave His all. He went much further than the second mile, and He did not look upon it as drudgery, but He gave Himself in infinite love.

43. Our Inner Drives — Servant or Master?

In each of us there are emotional drives that form an important element in the way we face life. These basic drives and inner urges demand of us some kind of response. We will either become master of these drives for the enrichment of our being, or we become slaves to them, making life difficult and ineffective.

Hunger and thirst are strong desires placed within us for our own good. They are needed for our survival. But the response to these desires will vary greatly. Those of us who must be on a diet know well the struggle and self-control it takes to resist the urge to eat. Some fail in their resistance, become a slave to the eating habit, and suffer the familiar consequences. The alcoholic has become a slave to the urge to drink.

Fear is also one of the indispensable elements in human nature. This too is needed for survival in an age like ours. The man who says that he has no fear is only fooling himself, for a person would not last long in a modern city, or driving through mountainous country, if he did not have some healthy fears.

CREATIVE FEAR

But fear is also a creative power in the human race. Our educational systems are inspired by the fear of ignorance as well as by the desire for learning. Industry has developed out of man's basic fear of poverty and want. Medical science has flourished because of man's innate fear of illness, pain, and death.

Fear can also be a destructive force in the personality. It all depends on what we do with our fears. They can become our master and make life miserable for us, or we can master fears so that they serve as an incentive for constructive and creative living. Fear can be master or slave, depending on our approach to it.

CURIOSITY

Curiosity is also a powerful drive. Man has a desire to know what is happening, and why. The little child gradually awakens to the world about him and always asks "why"? This curiosity can be a force for good, but it can also lead to evil. It has been a source of inspiration to the explorer, to the research scientist, and to every good student. It has sent men out on an endless search for new worlds to conquer. But it also becomes the basic desire that leads some to become Peeping Toms or inquisitive gossipers.

The urge to combativeness is often expressed in hard work or in the satisfaction of fighting for and defending a great truth. It has served to strengthen the handicapped person to face the frustrations of life with fortitude and courage. But it has been disastrous in the lives of those who develop chronic hatreds and hostilities, or in the person who lives with strong feelings of resentment.

SELF-ESTEEM

A sense of self-regard or self-esteem can also lead us both to good or to evil, depending on whether we are master or slave to the desire. It can lead a person to pride, selfishness, and avarice. It is common to see people in a devoted search for their own gains. But an adequate concept of self and a good sense of self-esteem is also an important part of character development, for a person with an inferiority complex cannot function at his best.

All these examples illustrate that the inner drives of personality must be mastered and used as basic ingredients for the Christian life. It is important to gain control of ourselves and of the urges that rise up in the human breast, for in them you see man at his best, or man at his worst.

Sin has also cast its long shadow on the inner man, so this will require a struggle. The inner life of man must be placed under the strong and powerful influence of the Holy Spirit. With earnest effort on our part, and a humble reliance on the indwelling Spirit, we too can make our inner drives our servant and not our master. For "he that ruleth his spirit, is better than he that taketh a city."

44. This "Busyness Complex"

It has become customary and fashionable to say that we are too busy. We all do this. The minister, the physician, the school teacher, the farmer, the mother in the home, and even the teen-ager in high school will join in the refrain "We are so very busy."

We often use this as an excuse, but it is not a very good one. We assume it as an attitude toward life and the passing of time. This is not wholesome for work, for because of it we tend to rationalize our lack of doing the things we don't really like to do.

I fear that this attitude is the result of our fretful, feverish way of going about our work. We rush around trying to do many things, but actually we accomplish none of them too well. It has often impressed me in conducting pastor's conferences in various areas that one of the common complaints of pastors is that they are too busy. This is true of ministers in smaller churches as well as those in larger ones. Often men who accomplish the most in broader Kingdom work are those who seem the least hurried.

I am inclined to feel that many people have developed a "Busyness Complex." It would be difficult to prove that we are more busy than our parents or grandparents. The marvels of modern transportation and the conveniences in our homes have given us many extra hours in which to do our regular work. Yet we are more rushed than ever before.

A DANGEROUS COMPLEX

A "busyness complex" is a dangerous complex. It leads not only to procrastination, broken appointments and forgotten promises, but also to poor mental health and bad work habits. It leads to mental, nervous, physical and spiritual stress.

Patients who come to the hospital often tell us that they broke down due to overwork. It is usually not the amount of work such people have done, but the emotional atmosphere in which they carried on their activities. It is not the external strain of too much work, but the internal stress that grows out of a faulty attitude toward time.

Time, in an objective sense, is a succession of minutes, hours, weeks, and years. God created everything in the setting of time. This is measured time, measured by clocks and calendars.

But the real essence of time is not found in a mere measured sequence of moments; it is found in the contents of these moments. The hour you spend in a hospital waiting room while a loved one's life hangs in the balance in the operating room is certainly much longer than an hour spent at a Christmas party. For some people the hour spent in church seems to be a long one.

BETTER PERSPECTIVE NEEDED

We need to gain a better perspective of time. The man with a "busyness complex" has placed himself under the tyranny of time. He has become a slave, and time is his master. He has allowed time to rule his life. He must learn instead to make time his slave.

People who must be in a hospital for a few months, or young men who are drafted into the service for a year or more, frequently consider these months as wasted months; as a period of time that is lost to them. But whether or not these are lost months depends upon our own attitude toward them. They could be months of spiritual enrichment and days of character development.

Another mistaken idea often expressed is that time heals all things. But time does not really heal. The wounds of sorrow or disappointment are healed by different processes in our emotional life and these processes operate in the framework of time. Time never forgave a single sin, though it may lead men to forget sin.

REDEEMING THE TIME

Paul tells us to "redeem the time," that is, to redeem it in the sense of buying up every opportunity it offers. Every moment must be brought to the great Giver of time.

I am convinced that with such an attitude toward time, we can lose much of this "busyness complex" and free ourselves from the strong hold that it has on us. Out in the free air, away from the prison of time, we must learn to say, "Time, thou art not my master, but my Master and thine dwells in the eternities."

45. A Healthy Attitude towards Work

Usually, when we meet a new patient at the hospital we ask, "What is your work?" An answer all too common is, "I just work in a factory. I have been running a machine for five years. There is not much chance for promotion in a job like that."

There is something frustrating in a remark like that. Much work today is of a routine nature. This is one of the hazards of modern mechanized industry. Men are required to perform the same detail day after day, year after year. This has been true in other occupations in days gone by. The man who digs ditches with pick and shovel, the farmer who works all day with fork or hoe, also belong in that class. Man is created to give expression to his own creativeness, but in such tasks he becomes a part of a machine.

But actually, it is not the kind of work in which we are engaged that endangers our mental and emotional health, it is the attitude we take toward it. When we begin to look upon our work as a dreary monotony, a necessary burden to be borne, we lose much of the joy of living. This may bring man to despair at human existence and cause him to be discontented with life.

There is a certain amount of routine in all work. The business man, the professional person, the secretary or the mother in the home, each has certain tasks that are monotonous. We all have work we would rather not do. The great question is, Can we take a healthy attitude towards such tasks?

A REBELLIOUS ATTITUDE

Some openly rebel at unpleasant duties. They are usually the persons who have never learned to do unpleasant things in their childhood and youth. Father or mother lifted the entire burden of such tasks. If the child did not feel like doing some bit of work that did not please him, he managed to get out of it.

The rebel against duty is a problem in society. He constitutes a real challenge for the teachers in school. He accounts for much of the absenteeism and job shifting in industry. He never seems to find his real place in life.

But there are more refined methods of rebelling. There is one that is becoming more and more common in our day. It is found in those who draw a strong contrast between work and pleasure. Work is considered to be a dreary monotony, a few hours of the day to be endured, but all during the day they look forward to the moments of pleasure when the work is done.

This is one of the incentives for pushing for shorter work weeks. It leads to an ever stronger urge to seek pleasure in both legitimate and illegitimate forms. There are millions who place work and pleasure in separate worlds.

The brief hours of pleasure must then have the power to raise the spirits so that the next day they can go back to their drudgery. No wonder such people become restless and discontented, for pleasure has a way of never being satisfied. The more we taste of it the more we need of it. Man needs ever stronger stimuli to gain satisfaction and this vicious cycle is hard to break.

A RESENTFUL ATTITUDE

There are many who do their work only because they must, but there is a spirit of resentfulness in the way in which it is done. Some are forever looking over the fence at others who seem to be so much better off than they are. They resent the authority of those who have been placed over them.

No one escapes situations in life in which we are compelled to do certain things we dislike to do. There are always certain burdens we would like to drop in mid-stream. There will be the stress of necessity, but it all depends upon our attitude toward this stress. Handel wrote *The Messiah* at a time when he was deeply in debt and was in danger of being thrown into jail because of it. But when you hear the "Hallelujah Chorus" you find no trace of resentment. It comes from a heart inspired by loftier motives.

I am sure that every minister has been told, "A minister really has a nice life, no hard work, and no clock to punch every morning." Most ministers will smile and say, "Yes, it is nice work." But they feel like saying, "Well, why didn't you become a minister, if it looks so good to you?"

THE SPIRIT OF RESIGNATION

Many faithful workers take the attitude of one who says, "You can't do anything about it, you might as well take it as it comes." With a strange self-pity they resign themselves to a drab and uneventful life. They feel that there is no use resisting so they just grin and bear it.

This happens to men in their work but also to mothers in a home. Burdened under the weight of household chores, they are "anxious and troubled about many things." But they nobly resign themselves to their lot in a pseudo-martyr's role. This can never be healthy for the mother and it does not inspire children.

A HIGHER PERSPECTIVE

Ministers love to tell the story about the three men who were engaged in building. When they were asked what they were doing, one man said, "I am laying bricks"; the other said, "I'm supporting my family"; the third, "I am building a cathedral." Men may do the same work but with a vastly different viewpoint in life.

The man who returns from his work and can thank God for work to do and the strength to do it has this insight. The husband and father who feels that his work is a means to a loftier goal, has gained that insight. There are fathers who have worked in factories all their lives just to be able to see their sons and daughters prepared for full-time kingdom work. There are mothers who have taken in washings so their sons might be ministers.

If you and I can think of our work as a means to a higher end, it will take out of it the sting of drudgery and we will see it as a blessing and a joy. We think then of the results of our toil in terms of an education for our children, a means to help a missionary in Africa, the gift of a Bible to a person in Formosa, or a means to help to lift the burden of a handicapped child. Then there is a compensation in work that no one can take from us.

46. Adaptability

At a pastors' conference a minister described one of his parishioners. "He is the kind of man for whom there are only two sides to any question, the one he holds, and the wrong one." There are such people. I am sure we all know one or two of them. They are so sure of their own viewpoint that they can see no other.

There is nothing so obnoxious as a person who thinks that he is always right, who never compromises, and who is happy when he can assert his own ideas in an argument. Some people may describe them as men of conviction, others will say that they are just plain stubborn. I suppose it depends on whether you agree with them or not.

Such people have a low level of adaptability.

RIGID THOUGHT PATTERNS

In our personal relationships with others we need a good deal of flexibility. When two people meet there are bound to be diffences, for no two people will ever think exactly alike on every issue. It is only normal for a husband and wife to have their differences, for children to differ with their parents, because each person has a right to his own opinions.

It is hard to live with a person who has extremely rigid thought patterns. Usually, rigidity of thinking is considered to be the mark of a strong personality. But actually, such attitudes towards others betrays an inner weakness, a feeling of insecurity. Such a person does not really dare to look at the other side of the issue.

The person who has nothing to feel threatened about in his dealings with others is not afraid to admit that he may be wrong and that there may be other sides to the question. He does not go around with a chip on his shoulder trying to defend his own viewpoint, but he feels that his views will stand on their own merit.

NARROW-MINDEDNESS

During a Presidential campaign we hear a lot of people speak with almost fanatical devotion to their own party. They have closed their minds to the fact that the other party may also have some good points, and that their own party may have a few weak spots.

Some people take this same view when it comes to the church. They feel that there is just one side to the question, and they prefer not to hear the other side. There is a tendency to classify people into two categories, either they are "with us" or they are "outsiders."

It always reminds me of the somewhat paranoid feelings of the Romans and the Greeks who considered all who were not of their own culture to be "barbarians."

In such a view of life the "I-We" relationship has weakened. It has become "I-we" instead of "I-WE." There is too much "I" and too little "WE."

BALANCED VIEWPOINT

We should try to keep the boat of life in balance, for if we shift our weight too much to one side or to the other we are liable to tip. We must not slip into the error of never having an idea of our own. A person who always agrees with you is a very poor friend. It is hard to converse with him, because there is little interplay of ideas and exchange of thought.

We need people who think for themselves. But we need a balance between the two extremes. The rigid person is in danger of intolerance and even bigotry. But the man who tries to be agreeable to everyone that comes along is liable to be a weak and spineless personality.

We need convictions upon which we can build our lives, we need standards by which we can live, but we must be willing to give and take on those matters of life that are not of great consequence. I am sure that you will agree that many of the differences in our homes, between parents and children, and even between members of a church, are not caused by matters of conviction, but by the little things that could well have been reconciled, if we were a bit more adaptable.

PAUL'S VIEW OF LIFE

None of us would consider the Apostle Paul as a man who could be easily swept along with the tide. He tells us "I am become all things to all men, that I may by all means save some." These words are sometimes applied unfavorably to people, especially to ministers. When it is said of them that "they are all things to all men" it is by no means intended as a compliment.

But Paul had learned to be at home in all classes of society. He had not gained this by reading *How to Win Friends and Influence People,* but he had learned this as a gift of grace, although I believe it was also a part of his native character.

He was a man of versatile sympathies. For, effective Christian living requires adaptability. We must learn to understand others and practice that understanding. We must learn to enter into the heart and life of others.

It depends upon the goal we have in mind. Paul's goal, "that I may win some," was a lofty one. We need the same goal in our lives. There is danger that we possibly may be more interested in tradition than in saving others. We may be critical rather than seeking to help others.

We may not sacrifice convictions for expediency, but we must learn to yield in a thousand little things so that we may be able to accomplish the great things of life. This involves humility and self-suppression. But it is worth it, if we may perchance win some.

Adaptability is a Christian virtue. Let's practice it.

47. Mountains and Molehills

Members of our hospital staff frequently say about a person who is ill with a mental depression, "Every molehill looks like a mountain to her." The lines of tension evident in the faces of these sufferers indicate the sad results of such an outlook on life. They lack the ability to see the events of life in proper proportion. However, these sick people cannot help themselves. This is but one of the symptoms of their illness, and no amount of argumentation can rid them of it.

But there are many of us who have our mountains and our molehills mixed up. Many tend to make mountains out of molehills, for this describes the fussy, timorous folks who magnify the trifles of life so that they seem to match the Rocky Mountains.

WORRISOME PEOPLE

The worrysome person does that. He looks at the road that lies ahead of him, and he feels that all the experiences will be mountainous ones. There may be some reason for concern, but most likely it is not a mountain but only a little heap of dirt that will be washed away by the next shower. The worrier always magnifies his difficulties, he loses the true measure of the magnitudes of life.

One of the tragedies of family life is also found in this approach to the events of life. When husbands and wives do not get along together, it is usually not due to some colossal evil that makes happiness impossible, but the cause of irritation is most likely some little things. These small provocations are then magnified to the point where the couple feels that they can no longer make a go of it. I have often observed that when something really big does come into their lives they see the folly of allowing the little foxes to spoil the marital vine.

Many of the troubles and disturbances among members in our churches are also of this nature. An older and wiser minister once suggested that the best way to resolve such difficulties is to have each party list their grievances in writing. When you lay the two papers side by side it usually reveals that in their anger they had really been magnifying trifles.

A LITTLE IRRITATION

Parents are often inclined to a similar spirit in dealing with their children. When a little boy breaks a window, or a little girl spills ink on the living room rug, it becomes an occasion for flying into a rage and stern disciplinary action. Often if that same son or daughter would become desperately ill, the parents would accept it with tranquility because they see the Lord's hand in it.

Yes, we make mountains out of molehills and in so doing we make both ourselves and those about us wretched. The real reason for this is that we have become petty and small, and we allow ourselves to be swept along by little things. We must learn to measure the true proportion of things in life more accurately, and learn to see the true value of the experiences of life. We must know that there are little things and there are big things, and we may not confuse the two.

One of the dangers of making mountains out of molehills is that it tends to bring us also to make molehills out of mountains. We become so nearsighted that we see the little things and fail to see the big ones. Basically, the worrying man, the petty soul, the man who is so concerned with trifles, has lost his view of the greatness of God. His concept of the majesty of the Creator has faded in the light of creature. Shrunken souls lose sight of the awesome things, they fail to see the mountain peaks of revelation, both in nature and in His Word.

PROPER PERSPECTIVE

If all throughout the week we have been magnifying the little things, it does not mean much for us to sing of the majesty of God on Sunday. We must not magnify the little things, but we dare not minimize the magnificent things. Our measure of life must be that the things that are great to God must also be great to us.

The prophet Jeremiah asks an interesting question of the people of his day when he says, "If thou hast run with footmen and they weary thee, then how canst thou contend with horses? and though in the land of peace thou art secure, yet how wilt thou do in the swelling of the Jordan?"

In other words, if we have failed in the lesser temptations of life, what are we going to do when the great temptations come? If we lose our tempers over minor irritations, how are we ever going to face a real test of patience?

If we mope and pine about the little aches and pains that come to us on life's pilgrimage, what are we going to do when serious illness comes? If we feel so bad about the loss of a few dollars, or the loss of some gain we had hoped to achieve, how can we expect to face with tranquility the loss of one whom we love most dearly?

If we fail so miserably in these little trials, how then will we do when we are called to cross the Jordan, or like Moses to climb to Nebo's lonely height?

See then how important it is in Christian mental health to measure life's true values and proportions. For when we make mountains out of molehills, how will we ever cross the mountains when we reach them?

48. A Martyr Complex

I suppose we all feel sorry for ourselves at times. It is a bad mental habit, one that leads to various emotional difficulties in life. As a rule, self-pity lays the blame for our difficulties upon others, and we tend to overlook our own faults. One extreme way of feeling sorry for ourselves is to develop a martyr complex.

I have met many people who suffer from this mental habit who are quite unaware of its existence. They have learned to magnify everything they do and experience in life. They feel that they are up against the greatest obstacles, for no one has ever had it quite as hard in life as they have. No one can possibly realize what they are going through.

When I counsel with people with a martyr complex, they will ask, "Did you ever go through something like this?" When I have to admit that I have not, they will smile with a knowing smile that tells me that I really don't know what I am talking about. No one can really understand the great load they are lifting.

Usually these self-styled martyrs will give the impression that they are bearing their cross with fortitude, and that they suffer in silence. But every action and gesture, and the expression on their face, indicates that they are very much dissatisfied with their lot in life. I sometimes wonder what happens when two people who have the same complex meet. I suppose they take turns denouncing friends, relatives, and fellow members of the human race, who fail to appreciate them.

THE BASIS

Usually a person that has such feelings is gripped with thoughts of personal inferiority. He is trying to get credit for possessing qualities of character which actually are absent. These people, in spite of their feelings of inferiority, desire recognition and approval. They want public acclaim, they crave affection. If they cannot obtain it by their accomplishments they will try to gain it by magnifying their sacrifices.

"I've worked my fingers to the bone for him," complains a wife, "but do you think he shows any appreciation for it?" She fails to note that she has been doing more than she was expected to do.

Being a wife and mother does not imply becoming a slave to the family. If a mother is a slave to her children, she is not being a good mother. She is doing things for her children which she should teach her children to do for themselves. She is really trying to enter too much into their lives, to live their lives for them.

MAGNIFYING SACRIFICES

I feel that sometimes we as ministers have also displayed a bit of the martyr spirit. Both missionaries and ministers have at times tended to magnify the sacrifices that have been made for the advantage of the church and kingdom. School teachers have not always been free from this same habit. This does not lend dignity to the professions, nor does it bring people to esteem them as highly as they should.

There are also people who feel that they are martyrs because they are defenders of principles. They claim that people dislike them because they stand strong on the great principles of faith and life. I find that often these are people who have the capacity of getting themselves into difficulty, or getting themselves disliked because of their personal attitudes. It is often the way the principles are promoted, rather than the principles themselves.

I am sure there are other examples of these self-styled martyrs. They are willing to work hard, endlessly, for another person, or for a cause. They do this because they actually crave acceptance and love. They feel that they will be admired by others when they do more than is expected of them. This would also be the case, if they did not, alongside of their work, develop a martyr spirit. This often spoils the good they try to do. For in the spirit of the martyr is a certain amount of aggressiveness which makes them unacceptable to others.

No one likes to be reminded of the sacrifices that others are making for him. When parents often remind their children of the great sacrifice they are making for them, in providing for care and clothing, in giving an education, they will not thereby instill greater love and admiration in them. This is trying to buy affection, and love cannot be bought at any price.

HOW TO OVERCOME

How then can we overcome this mental habit? I have found that it is important for people with a martyr complex to learn to see the folly of their attitude. It is well that they recognize that no one in life is indispensable. When the Lord suddenly takes a parent out of the family circle, the survivors will get along. Our work will go on, for others stand ready to take over where we leave off.

We cannot live another's life for him. We sometimes try, and soon find that this is not appreciated. Each person must learn to live his own life, and strive to find satisfaction in fulfilling his task as best he can.

But basic to the martyr complex is also the wrong attitude toward God. For when we feel that the Lord has dealt bitterly with us, that our lot in life is such a difficult one, we are actually complaining against God.

This implies a rebellion against the sovereign authority of a loving God. Jesus teaches us the lesson that when we have done all that we have been commanded to do, we must still confess that we are "unprofitable servants."

49. Alcohol Is Not the Answer

The fact is undeniable that drinking is becoming an ever increasing problem in the church. Frequently we see some of the results of excessive drinking in those who are admitted into our mental hospitals.

There are today more drinkers in our country than ever before. Sixty-four per cent of adult Americans imbibe. There are 65 million persons that can be classified as "social drinkers," over 20 million of these are women. One social drinker out of every 15 will some day become an alcoholic.

There are 3 million "problem drinkers" in our country. There are the people who periodically get into difficulty because of overuse of alcohol. There are 750,000 chronic alcoholics in the U.S. Each day 175,000 persons lose work because of intoxication. Problem drinkers have three times as many accidents as the non-drinker, in fact they are the cause of 10 per cent of all automobile accidents.

THE RESULTS OF EXCESSIVE DRINKING

Alcohol is both a drug and a food. In moderate quantities it serves as a stimulant, in excessive amounts it serves as a depressant. This explains some of its medicinal qualities. When a man drinks a cocktail before his meal, it gives him a sense of well-being. It serves as an emotional sedative.

But excessive drinking leads a person to feel low and depressed. This accounts also for the "hangover" that is experienced after a drinking bout. When this is carried on for a period of time, alcohol will destroy some of the useful tissues of the body, especially of the brain. This accounts for many of the cases on "skid row" and in mental institutions.

The worst agony that I have ever seen any person suffer in all these years in a mental hospital is that of a man who was in a state of "delirium tremens." In such a case there are hallucinations that cause indescribable suffering.

If any young person is tempted by drink, I would like to show him a person who has suffered these tragic results of the over-use of alcohol. I am sure that he would think twice before drinking to excess.

In spite of these evident facts 3 million Americans go on drinking to excess. It causes untold havoc to the human brain and organism, it leads to tragic suffering in the homes of the drinkers, and yet, there are more drinkers today than ever before.

WHY DO PEOPLE DRINK TO EXCESS?

Basically, the excessive drinker is a childish person. He faces life in an infantile way. When a little baby cries mother will give him a pacifier. When a boy stubs his toe he find solace in a lollipop. The full-grown man has his problems and he finds relief in a bottle of whisky.

Such people are running away from reality, especially the things that seem unpleasant to them. They use alcohol as a means to assuage the mental pain caused by personal misfortune of one form or another. This is, of course, only temporary relief, for alcohol is not the answer to such problems, it only tends to deepen them and make them worse. It adds a new problem to life.

It is true, there are some people that are afflicted with some forms of emotional illness, and they can find relief for the time in drink. But always, alcohol does not give real or lasting relief, it only tends to make the emotional disturbance worse.

The deeper cause for drinking lies within the human heart. The excessive drinker is basically a selfish person. He gains attention by his drinking. He is not concerned about the embarrassment and discomfort that he may cause his mate, he thinks only of his own pleasure and satisfaction.

IS IT SIN OR SICKNESS?

There is much discussion today as to whether excessive drinking is sin or sickness. The theory that it is an emotional illness is preached rather loudly today. There is some truth in it. The alcoholic is indeed an emotionally disturbed person.

But this does not mean that it is not a sin. A man may have a basic personality weakness, but this does not imply that his actions are not to be judged by the laws of God and the teachings of the Bible.

I do not feel that I have to answer the question, "Is it sin or is it sickness?" for all life's actions have a moral quality to them. They also have emotional aspects to them. Looking at these two aspects of the matter of drinking, it can be both sin and an emotional disturbance.

A man may be emotionally unstable, insecure and his reactions to life may be on a childish level so that he cannot resist drink.

This may explain his actions, but it does not excuse him. Before God he is guilty.

But I do not feel that I may condemn him. For I too have the same drives, the same impulses, if it were not for the restraining grace of God I could also be an alcoholic, and so could you. So when I talk to him, I do not condemn him, I try to accept him as a person with a deep emotional problem, but even more, as one with great spiritual needs. He needs help in his emotional problems, but even more, he needs to know the forgiving love of the Savior. He needs the inner strengthening power of the Holy Spirit, for this alone can keep him on the road to sobriety.

I am convinced that no man can conquer the craving for alcohol unless he learns to lean on the Power that is from above.

No, alcohol is not the answer. But a strong, vital and positive faith is.

50. Cultivating Happiness

In every community and congregation there are people who have a sad and dejected appearance. There is a tragic look in their eye, and it would seem that it might hurt them if they would smile or laugh. They are the gloom-chasers, the people who are perpetually unhappy. They can tell you all about the accidents that have happened, about the people who have cancer and other serious illnesses, for they seem to enjoy being sad.

It is true that anyone who would pretend to tell people that he has ways and means by which they can always be happy would be a fool. There is no way for any one of us perpetually to see the bright side of life and never to see the dark side. In the course of every life there are tragic experiences. But when a person is always unhappy, or when the prevailing tone of life is sad, there is something wrong.

ACUTE UNHAPPINESS

The dictionary defines the term "unhappy" as: "sad; miserable; wretched; sorrowful." Acute unhappiness usually consists of a feeling of sadness and irritation or regret due to the fact that a person is not getting what he wants, or he is getting something that he does not want. It is not the actual experience that makes a person feel dejected, it is the attitude he takes toward the frustrating experience.

In an imperfect world we cannot expect always to be happy. But we can do much to conquer a sour and sad disposition.

Much of the unhappiness seen in people grows out of inner anger or disappointment. These emotions are negative ones, and negative emotions create unhappiness. I have met a person who felt most unhappy because she felt that she needed the approval of a friend who turned a cold shoulder toward her. I could well understand why, for no one likes to share the company of a gloomy person. I have met several people who were most unhappy because they could not satisfy their own perfectionist ideals. Such people are usually angry at themselves.

CHRONIC UNHAPPINESS

When a person feels unhappy for an extended period of time, it is well for him to ask himself why he is so unhappy. Usually, when we see the cause, the real cause, we are better able to overcome. There is no good cause for being perpetually unhappy. Even coming from the setting of an unhappy home is not sufficient reason for trying to carry on this same spirit into the next generation. Sometimes people need personal help to overcome their unhappiness.

A person can cultivate the art of being happy. It is utterly foolish to be forever chasing the gloom, for we can change our attitudes so that we can also see the rainbow in the clouds. This does require discipline of self, but it is a worth-while goal.

PLEASANT ATMOSPHERE

Our homes should be pleasant places in which to live. The music of hearty laughter should be heard there. There should be more smiles than frowns. It is not healthy for children to be reared in an atmosphere of sadness. It is not healthy for parents either. Since happiness is an attitude we take toward life, it is something over which we do have control.

I am not thinking of an artificial kind of gladness, or a Pollyanna view of life. The forced smile is not very convincing. But the Bible shows us the way when it tells us repeatedly to "be of good cheer." For happiness flows from the heart. Where true happiness dwells, the undercurrent of this spirit can be felt in a home, even in a time of great loss and sorrow.

Too often people will gain the impression that all Christians are unhappy people, and that ministers and elders should not laugh. There are those who feel that religion is something sad and gloomy. Christianity does have its sad moments, but it is basically a religion of joy and inner happiness. The long face and unsmiling lips do not bring a vibrant witness to the world of our day. There are too many unhappy people in the world. The Christian should show that his viewpoint of life is one of hope and optimism. Cultivate this spirit of happiness, for it is the mark of a healthy Christian life.

51. Talking Things Over

Many tense people, when they get into a stew about something that bothers them, will withdraw and brood about their problem. Instead of bringing it out into the open, they keep it bottled up inside. In this way trifling matters often seem like major problems, and molehills look like mountains. The more they fret about their situation, the more they are filled with anxiety and fear.

This indicates that a person who is in the grip of an upsetting emotion is not in a good position to solve his problem because he cannot think straight. He does not see things in their proper light. When our feelings are upset, it's hard to face life objectively, for we color our outlook on life in the light of the prevalent mood.

The best thing to do in such situations is to talk things over with someone else. This does not mean that you blurt out your private matters to any person who happens to be within hearing distance. This would only make matters worse. A mother who talked over the problems in her marriage with teen-age daughters multiplied her problem, because it also upset her children.

CONFIDENTIAL RELATIONSHIPS

Find someone in whom you can have confidence, someone whom you feel can give you adequate support and help. It may be that you need a strong shoulder on which to cry, or it may be one who treats you with firmness and sets you straight. But sharing a problem with one whom you trust helps to lighten the load that you carry in your own heart.

The relief you find in sharing a problem may well spring back to the days when, as a child, you came to your mother or father with every hurt finger or injured feeling. The pain was removed as by magic under the influence of a soothing word or a gentle touch. There is power in the warmth of human sympathy that often surpasses the power of drugs.

Some people have a feeling that seeking help is a sign of weakness. Actually, it is a sign of strength. Those who try to solve their problems alone are afraid to admit that they could have a problem. People who act so brave and tough on the outside are often the ones who need help most.

VERBALIZING YOUR PROBLEM

When you talk things out with someone, you have an opportunity to see your problem in a different light. Just to tell your story to someone else forces you to put it into words – to define it. When you must reconstruct the situation that brought on your problem, you have often taken the most important step toward its solution. Fears often begin to look silly when you tell others about them. People often say, "It must seem ridiculous to you, but it bothers me."

When we do not have an outlet for our tensions, they seem to become bottled up and we do well to find a good safety valve. You may be very angry at someone, and your anger might become worse if you talk to the person you hate. But when you talk about these hostile feelings to an understanding friend, you can express your anger safely, and possibly you can rid yourself of it.

Talking things over often opens the road for a sensible course of action. Usually we must develop some plan, or make some decision that will help us out of our difficulties.

NOT OUR DEPENDENCY

It is true that some people become quite dependent upon the person whom they accept as their counselor. It is not good to let other people solve your problems. It is far better to work together at the problem and then derive a mutually-agreed-upon solution.

Parents often complain that their children do not come to them for counsel and advice. They often do not talk things over with them. There may be some good reasons for this. Too often parents are emotionally involved with the problems the children face.

It is good to note that more and more people turn to their pastors for help. Some people find it more helpful to talk things over with a doctor. Some find help by talking to a friend or a relative. People are usually more than ready to share in other people's problems and troubles. But whatever you do, do not keep things bottled up where they will produce tensions.

But above all, talk things over with God. He is always ready to listen, willing to help us, and able to make all things work out for good.

52. You Never Win an Argument

A man came to his office looking rather dejected. When asked what was wrong, he said, "I had an argument with my wife." When asked who had won, he confessed, "Well, I won, but I can't say that I feel very good about it." He well knew that he had left his wife in tears, and he went on through the day feeling tense and irritable. For no one really wins an argument. You may make your point, may even have silenced your opponent, but you pay for it in the strain and tension you carry with you.

There is plenty of room for friendly discussion, for there are differences of opinion among people. But arguments usually develop a feeling of anger or hostility. Too often friendly discussions end in angry debates. Such sessions between husband and wife, or between parents and children, often disrupt family relationships.

ARGUMENTATIVE PEOPLE

Some people can argue about the most insignificant subjects. The Greeks had a reputation for that kind of thing. Such persons have argumentative natures. They have learned to like to present opposing viewpoints, and then will belabor some little point to convince others that they are right and others are wrong. It gives them a feeling of having conquered a victim.

Most likely the defiant and obstinate have a basic need to be that way. In spite of their words and outward attitudes, they have feelings of inferiority. It would threaten them if they had to admit that they might be wrong.

Two little boys argue on a "'t is" and "'t aint" basis. They keep at it till one or both of them get tired of it. Much of adult discussion is on the same basis. Two opposing views are presented, and each is unwilling to listen to the other's view. Each is unwilling to admit that the position of the opponent might have some validity, and the discussion does not come to a conclusion, except that each will conclude that the other is just plain stubborn.

AN OPEN MIND

Arguments usually produce more heat than light. They create more tensions than solutions. Usually the emotions are too much involved. Actually, the truth will most likely lie somewhere between the two extreme positions. For this reason it is good to approach a discussion with the thought that you may be mistaken.

Such an approach means that we are willing to re-examine our position with an open mind. It is only the petty and the threatened person who is afraid that he might be wrong.

I am convinced that parents will often have to admit to their children that they were mistaken. I know some parents are very reluctant to do this because they feel that this will undermine their authority. But children will respect their parents more if they hear them admit that they could be wrong, or even that they had a mistaken view of things. A teacher or a minister need not be afraid to admit that he was mistaken. After all, no human being ever has encyclopedic knowledge.

DISCUSSING AND WITNESSING

This does not mean that we have to take a wishy-washy approach to life. The Christian is one who will have firm opinions and convictions. There are truths he will not surrender, and spiritual principles that he will not water down. But these are not subjects that come up for arguments. We may discuss Christianity, but we do not argue it. We are to be witnesses to the truth. When we start to argue, we have already lost.

The man of strong convictions need not be fearful and suspicious. We need not build up tensions by heated arguments. Be a positive witness to your convictions, for in this way you can be of the greatest influence on others. It's only when you have a weak point that you have to substantiate it with arguments. But in the argument you are bound to lose, for no one really wins an argument.

53. Living without Appreciation

Mother has prepared a meal for the family. Every member eats heartily, but when the meal is over, they move away from the table without saying, "That was a good meal, Mom." The children even try to get out of doing the dishes. Mother may well remember the times when they were critical of some of the food she had prepared, and so she does not feel too bad.

This is a common happening in life; it's inexcusable, to be sure. Life would be much smoother and more pleasant if there were more appreciation and gratitude. But if mother reacts to this lack of recognition by feeling unwanted and a little depressed, she, too, is showing a lack of maturity. Modern psychology tells us that people who have a strong craving for praise and acclaim are lacking in security. They have not grown up.

DESIRE FOR RECOGNITION

This desire for recognition and attention is very strong in children, and they make use of many devices to get it. But as we grow up we no longer need it in such large doses. We all still have a need of some recognition, but we do not feel too bad if it is not given. Most mothers will feel that their meal was a success if every member ate it with relish.

Are you one of the people who needs public acclaim for what you do? What is going to happen to you if it is withdrawn, or forgotten? Will it make you bitter, or give you a feeling of being unwanted and unimportant? The fact is that many of us will have to learn to live without it. All of us have times when our best efforts slip by unnoticed by others. The real mark of mature character and endurance is that we can keep on plodding along, doing our best work, even though we do not hear words of gratitude.

Often the best efforts of people are not recognized. The work of many of the great artists was unheralded until they left this earthly scene. Some of the great composers of music died in poverty. We have often read of the greatness of Helen Keller, but few people know the name of Anne Sullivan Macy, the little lady whose selfless devotion made it possible for Miss Keller to do the things she did.

It is good to recognize that many of our best efforts are not met with gratitude and appreciation. But this should not stop us from doing them. This should not make us bitter, nor make us feel insecure. We must rise above this level and find satisfaction in doing the things we do for the very fact that we feel they are worth while and important.

INNER SATISFACTION

Learn to live with this lack of appreciation. Develop the mental attitude of not seeking the praise of men. You must live with your own conscience, regardless of what others may say or think. The best efforts give a mature person an inner satisfaction that he will not allow a lack of appreciation to take away from him. The only praise a mature person needs is the feeling that he has done his best. He will rise above the whims and fancies of the crowd.

If you, in your own heart, are not sure that you are doing your best, you will need a large measure of appreciation from others. If you feel insecure in your accomplishments, you will need constant encouragement. But if you can face your work with confidence, you can move ahead without the appreciation of others.

Since we live in a world where there is often a lack of recognition, the Christian finds a higher sense of satisfaction in the knowledge that the Father in heaven sees and knows what he is doing. The prospect of hearing him say, "Well done," is abundant compensation for the thanklessness of our fellow men. Jesus saw and recognized the few mites of the widow, as she placed them in the temple treasury. He said of Mary, "She has done what she could." With such higher recognition we can well learn to live without the acclaim of men.

54. Christian Enthusiasm

"My husband never gets excited about a thing, you can't even make him angry." This is a complaint that is often heard from wives when they describe their husbands. Men also voice this complaint when they speak of their wives. "I wish she could get enthusiastic about something in life, she seems so lifeless and has lost her pep."

It is a well-known fact that there is a vast difference in people as far as the spark of vitality is concerned. Some seem to be effervescent and sparkling, others are stoical and unmoved. Those who lack enthusiasm often express a bored attitude.

This is not all due to physical vitality. I know some invalids who have a wide range of interests and pursue them with great zest. There are athletes, with a good deal of physical vitality, who are bored with life. Usually you will find that it is due to an attitude toward life which has developed.

CHILDISH ENTHUSIASM

People are born with enthusiasm. Little children can get very excited about many things. When they get a new toy, or find a new playmate, they can bubble over with wonderful delight. It is true, such enthusiasm can get out of bounds. A little boy insisted on taking his new tricycle with him to his bedroom, and early in the morning he disturbed the family by riding it in his room.

This is normal childish enthusiasm. But it must be curbed for it cannot be allowed to have unbridled expression. It is something emotional and has few intellectual restraints. As parents, we sometimes bridle this enthusiasm too much. We approach it too negatively. If a child is slapped down every time he shows his exuberance, he will soon find that it does not pay to get excited. When this is done too often he loses his intense drive for living.

It is normal when we mature, that we lose some of the extreme emotional enthusiasm of youth. Sometimes we tend to keep some of the childish interests. There are women who never lose their childish interest in clothes. It has often been said about a man with a new car, "He is like a youngster with a new toy." These are remnants of childish enthusiasm carried over into adult life.

TEEN-AGE ENTHUSIASM

Young people can usually generate a great deal of vitality and pep. You can hear it in the deafening shouts when the high school team is winning a close basketball game.

This too is normal. The teen-ager who loses his enthusiasm too early is walking in dangerous emotional pathways. It is not good to develop a sophisticated attitude that is resolved never to show any excitement or emotion.

During their developing years young people should lose some of their childish enthusiasm, and develop new interests in life. The eagerness of youth must grow up and be tempered and shaped by experience, judgment and a sense of humor. The joy of life must then be sought not in the satisfactions of the moment, but in the achievements of years of struggle and work.

LOST ENTHUSIASM

The lives of many people are like the river Rhine which has its beginnings in the turbulent Alpine streams, and then runs more and more slowly, until we can hardly detect which way the current flows. Sometimes the experiences of life contribute to this. I know a young lady who has lost both her parents, has been sent from one aunt to another, has been rudely rejected by a young man, and has been frustrated in many of her efforts to succeed in life. She has lost most of her drive for living, her enthusiasm has waned.

There comes a time in nearly every life when the fundamental drive for adventure begins to wane. The radiance begins to dull. It can come when the youngest child is married. It may be at the time of retirement from work. It can come on when we realize that much of life's span has been spent, and yet we have accomplished so little.

At such a time we should stir ourselves to develop new interests to give expression to more radiant living. There is always the danger of becoming bored. For the mind is by nature lazy and does not like to be disturbed by new adventures of thought.

It is a wonderful thing to see older people still living on with gusto, taking a lively interest in the family, in the nation and in the church.

SPIRITUAL ENTHUSIASM

You may not get excited about the coming of a new grandchild, or the election of a new president, but we may never lose our enthusiasm for the blessings of the spiritual life. Woe to the person who can no longer thrill to the reading of Psalm 46, or the strains of the Hallelujah Chorus.

There are many bored people in our age. Many have lost their sense of childish wonder and even a more mature sense of awe for spiritual things. These have lost their enthusiasm, for the word *enthusiasm* comes from *en-theos,* God in us. It means to be possessed by God. The fire of the indwelling Spirit should stir the soul to a sense of wonder and amazement as we behold the blessings of his grace.

Our Lord still says to the spiritually unenthusiastic, "So because thou art lukewarm, and neither hot nor cold, I will spew thee out of my mouth."

55. Courage for Daily Living

The basic training of our armed forces includes a great deal of rugged exercise to put the body in shape for the strenuous life of military service. Due to the fact that many who enter the service are in poor physical shape, an increasing emphasis has been placed on the physical fitness of youth. In our culture, we have a tendency to become soft and flabby.

Due to the emotional impact of modern warfare, a new and important element has been added. This is psychological training. Young men must be prepared also for psychological warfare and, if possible, for the destructive brain-washing techniques employed by some of our enemies. It has become important to attempt to instill great courage and resistance in situations of danger.

This is the kind of courage all need today, for there are many situations that demand the ability to stand up and fight. Courage is defined as that quality of mind that enables one to meet danger and difficulties with firmness. It implies stability of mind and purpose, and the casting aside of undue fears.

LACK OF COURAGE

Too often we think of courage only when we come face to face with some great obstacle, or some great disappointment. But the real evidence of courage is seen in everyday life. It takes courage to live, to face the ups and downs of life as they come to us. It takes real staying power to live one day at a time.

Our streamlined culture with its luxuries is not conducive to building strong bodies. That is why physical fitness is being emphasized. But our age is not a good age for training children and young people in developing courage. It is so easy to spoil our children. Too often we show our love and concern for them by giving them all they desire. There is a real danger of overprotectiveness, and this does not help them to become "profiles in courage."

This is true for all of us in our time. We are given protection by a paternalistic state in every eventuality of life. We have social security, health insurance, unemployment insurance, protection in old age; in virtually every area of life we are protected. This has become a necessity, but it does not serve to build up a strong and courageous nation.

SOURCES OF INNER STRENGTH

How then can we build courage in ourselves and in our children in such a time as this? This is not something that can be learned in ten easy lessons. The evidence or the lack of courage lies deeper within the individual. It touches the inner source of strength upon which we can draw when the going becomes difficult. It is the ability to use the inner resources that God has placed in each of us, and to use them constructively in daily contacts.

It is not only the great crises that call forth this strength, but the daily routine of living. You can soon know the measure of courage that a man has when you live with him, or when you work next to him in the office or shop. You see the courage of people in the way they go about their work, and the ability to stand up under the day-by-day battle of life. We see its absence or presence in the way they meet sickness or unemployment or temptation. It is seen in the measure of stability with which people walk life's daily road.

Courage demands that we have purpose and goal. It requires that we have a set of values that we want to attain. It means that we desire to gain these purposes so strongly that we are willing to face any obstacle that stands in the way. It is this that is often lacking in the man who lacks courage.

To find the courage to live, set before you a lofty goal. This should not be hard for the Christian, for the very essence of the Christian faith is that it reaches out to that which lies ahead. Paul expressed the secret of his courage in the night of the shipwreck when he said, "Whose I am, and whom I serve." This is the courage we all need for daily living.

BRIDGING THE GENERATIONS

Man, that is born of a woman
is of few days, and full of trouble.

He cometh forth like a flower
and is cut down.

He fleeth also as a shadow
and continueth not. –

Seeing his days are determined
and the number of his months is with Thee;
And Thou hast appointed his bounds
that he cannot pass.

Job 14

56. Becoming an Ancestor

The words *grandfather* and *grandmother* call to mind a picture of a lovable couple who have grown old together. I can well remember visiting at the home of my grandparents. I looked upon them with a feeling of something short of veneration. Along with the rock candy and "pink peppermints" they represented a mature outlook upon life and a seasoned faith. The toil-wearied hands gave evidence of having lived a full life, and their ready smile indicated that they were not afraid of being old.

One day a granddaughter was born into our family. Now it all looks different. I do not feel a bit like the portrait I have of my own grandparents, and I hope that the new branch on the family tree does not look at me in the same way I looked at them.

Quite naturally, grandparents rejoice in their grandchildren and observe with mounting satisfaction their progress, both physical and mental. They often shower these youngsters with debilitating tenderness. Many a mother can testify that it takes a few weeks to bring little Jane or Peter back to normal again, after they have basked for a few days in the fond attention of grandmother and in the indulgence of grandfather.

A baby is always fascinating; this is even more so when there is the bond of blood ties. I dare say there are more grandmothers who carry pictures of their grandchildren in their purses than there are mothers who carry pictures of their youngsters. I suppose this is due to the fact that we can claim them as our own, and yet we are not required to do all the routine tasks that their care requires.

CHANGING PATTERNS

There are many people today who become grandparents in their early or middle forties, some are great grandparents in their sixties. It is not so unusual to see pictures of five generations together. This is due to the fact that there are many early marriages, and also that people live longer than in previous times. It brings together a wider span of generations living at the same time.

This leads to a changing concept. The typical grandmother of days gone by is illustrated well in a painting such as Whistler's "Mother." This portrait hardly fits today. We have all seen grandmothers, well covered with cosmetics, smoking a cigaret, leading a few grandchildren down the street, and they have a hard time keeping up with her. Grandfather can still play ball with his grandsons. This is quite a different picture from what we saw 50 years ago.

Resulting from this changing concept has also been a loss of esteem for the previous generation. In countries like Mexico, and many of the European lands, the older generation is honored and even placed in esteem. In our own land, and in our present generation there is not only a gap between the generation, but even a conflict. This striving for individualization is not wholesome, for it tends to break the feeling of belonging to the chain of the generations.

A LINK IN THE CHAIN

Oliver Wendell Holmes once wrote that "heredity is like an omnibus in which all our ancestors are packed." We form but a link in the chain. We are like people running in a relay race. We take our place in the race of life for a span, and then we hand the torch into the hands of the next runner in the course, and so it moves on.

This brings to us a challenging and humbling thought. Through our heritage, our influence and training of our children, we leave our traces not just in the next generation, but also in our children's children, throughout the generations. The thought could be overwhelming, if we did not remember the gracious promises of our Lord.

There is something thrilling as we stand as grandparents to see this new little bundle of life. We think of the marvelous possibilities in this child, either for good or for evil. We marvel at the potentials which are found in that little brain and in those tiny hands. And we wonder what influence we have left that can be carried on through the generations to come.

We cannot help but think of the possible dangers that threaten. Will this little one have to face some of the devastating results of the terrible weapons which our generation has produced? What about the great load of national debt which our generation is making, will the generation to come have to pay for this?

We see the sinking of the moral level of the people of our time, are we leaving a world in which it will be hard for a Christian to live? And what about the spiritual heritage which we leave for those that follow us? Will the church, which this generation will in due time leave behind, be the kind of church in which we desire our grandchildren to have a part?

Becoming an ancestor has its joys, but it also brings its responsibilities. Are we living up to them?

57. In Moments of Sorrow

As members of the family we stood around the coffin of our brother who had slipped away from us through the narrow door of death. We had been prepared for this day, for we had seen it coming from the distance as it crept upon us with unrelenting pace. He had suffered much agonizing pain, so for him it was a sweet release from suffering. But he was still in the strength of life when the diagnosis of cancer came to him and told him that his days would not be many.

There are many thoughts that press themselves into the foreground when a loved one is called home. There are questions we cannot answer and problems we cannot solve. Why should one who was still needed in his family circle be taken, when others live on for whom life has become a heavy burden? Why should the Lord consider that his work on earth was so suddenly completed?

MEMORIES

There are many memories that come to mind. And there are also feelings of regret. If we had known that this would happen, we might have treated each other a bit more kindly at times. We might not have spoken words that hurt; we would have shown more love, more interest. But this, too, is a part of the normal course of life and human relations. Most of us have feelings of self-judgment and guilt when we have lost someone who is close to us. But we cannot turn back the clock of time.

When death comes after long illness, our minds and hearts have been somewhat prepared for it. We stood at the bedside of our brother often and saw the cancer eating away at his mind that once was keen and alert. We watched life ebb slowly from his body, and there was a strange feeling of helplessness. Words often seemed empty at such a time, nor were they really needed. But when death strikes there is still a suddenness and a painful finality about it. For man was born to live, not to die.

But actually, we need not mourn for him. He left behind a testimony of faith and a life filled with loving service and devotion to his Lord. A man shows his true self when the mind is clouded and the conscious shell no longer functions and the inner thoughts seem to come to expression. Often in these moments he was in prayer, when many a person might have cursed the awful pain.

A PERSONAL LOSS

In times of sorrow we experience sufferings that are caused by a personal loss. Painfully you must let go of the past and set your mind to the future. It seems more bleak and empty for a while, but this is something we learn to accept. We are sad because we have been deprived. We ache because we suffer separation. This is something with which we all must live sooner or later, for death is as much a part of life as is birth and growth and the aging process.

We know, too, that the wound will again heal itself, sometimes more slowly than at other times. But within us there is a source of strength that enables us to face life, and also the eventual reality of death. For in such moments the spiritual resources that are within enable us to look up and to look ahead. We gain somehow a feeling of the deeper meaning of life, and we face its challenges in a more vibrant way. It tells us that life's day is rather short and that we must make the best of every moment.

SPIRITUAL RESOURCES

There are resources for meeting grief. They develop in the life of the Christian, and when we need them we can put them to use. For the faith and the courage that we need for facing life is the same that we need for facing death. For our faith is not just an antidote for sorrow, but an incentive for better and more consecrated living.

So the wounds of sorrow and of grief heal again, and we find that God has many lessons to teach us while the wounds are healing. When we seek only for comfort, we do not really find it. But grief can bring a new understanding of self, a richer sympathy for others, and a greater incentive for Christian living. This is creative sorrow. This is, by God's grace, Christian sorrow. It has not been sent in vain.

58. Aid for the Grieving

When death enters a family, there will be a feeling of sorrow, an emotional pain that must be healed before a person can again live comfortably. There is nothing unchristian about expressing grief. God has made man so that he can bear the shock of grief, even when it strikes with sudden swiftness. One of the means that helps a person to overcome in such crises is the ability to express his emotions by means of tears and other expressions of grief.

Often the people who cannot cry suffer most deeply inside because they are not able to express their feelings adequately. A highly emotional person will often express grief more intensely, but will also recover more quickly.

NORMAL GRIEF

Normal grief proceeds with decreasing intensity as the days and weeks wear on. After a time the world will again seem to be a less painful place in which to live, and the person will return to a normal way of living.

There are various ways in which a person can be helped in times of grief.

A very common custom in our community is to have the body of the deceased lie in state in a funeral home. The relatives will be present at certain announced hours, and friends will then come to view the remains and express sympathy to the grieving ones. In some cases this is extended for several days so that the relatives are thoroughly fatigued by the time the funeral is conducted. As a result of this practice, very few people attend the funeral, which is usually conducted in a funeral parlor.

FUNERAL CUSTOMS

I am still partial to having a funeral conducted in a church. A good deal of the religious dignity of the funeral service is lost in the somber surroundings of a funeral parlor. When a person has worshiped for many years in a given church, it would seem fitting to have these services in the same place. True, it is not a service of worship, but it is a religious activity in which the Word of God has a central place.

It is often interesting to listen to the comments that are made to the bereaved. People will express their sympathy and tell how much they respected the departed friend. A very common remark that is added is, "He looks very natural." This is, of course, rarely true, for when life is removed from the body, it has lost its naturalness.

Another statement that gives little comfort is, "He is much better off now; you would not really wish him back." This remark does not give much comfort, nor is it always true; for the loved ones might well wish him back. It is far more important that a grieving person recognize the fact that the loved one is indeed gone, and that the earthly ties have been broken and that normal relationships cannot be restored.

RELEASE FROM SORROW

Before the grieving process is complete, those who remain will have to be freed from the image of the deceased person. As long as the image of the person is constantly before them, they have not been released from sorrow.

Nor must we rest in the illusion that one day, when we meet again in heaven, the normal relationships of life will be restored. There are better resources God has given us to aid in the time of grief — the assurance that the God who has taken a loved one from our side is the same God who will walk by our side as we face the future and strive to readjust our way of living. It is the confidence that He will not leave us in our moments of sorrow, but that He has a comfort that counterbalances all of life's inner pain.

For this is the faith that "mourns not as those who have no hope," but that rests in the one who revealed himself as the resurrection and the life. Rather than to tell a sorrowing person that the loved one who has been called home looks natural, point them to the source of comfort that flows from the Victor over death, whose aid will not fail them as they face the future. Assure them of your concern and your prayer for an abiding comfort, for this gives genuine help.

59. The Passing of a Generation

Recently the members of our family stood beside the open grave of our mother. She had lived a full and rich life, for the Lord had allowed her to celebrate her 85th birthday. It was not a sad occasion, for she had prayed that the Lord would take her and release her from her suffering. It is not so much a time of grieving as a time of memories and introspection.

We had been privileged to have mother for many years, and she exerted her influence upon her daughter and five sons. She was proud of her family, ever rejoicing in the fact that they served her Lord and the church she so genuinely loved.

DIFFICULT DAYS

The years she spent in the manse were very different from the present time. Many of those years were still in the horse-and-buggy days, in the days of mud roads and coal stoves. But she enjoyed those years in the service of the church, even though there were sacrifices and personal inconveniences. She recognized them as a challenge and put her heart and soul into them.

One by one she saw her children leave. A boy of seven was plucked from her heart by a dread disease. Other members of the family went off to school, and then one after the other chose a life's mate and left the family home. Almost three decades ago my father was taken from her side, but she marched serenely on throughout the years, until she quietly slipped away.

A LINK IN A CHAIN

The course of life moves relentlessly on. As we stood at the grave we felt that this was the passing of a generation. This link in the chain of the generations had slipped beyond the veil, and now we form the next link. From her frail and toil-worn hand she has placed the lighted torch in our hands, and we, in turn, are to pass it on to younger hands.

She left behind a priceless heritage, the kind of influence we would in turn like to give our children. There was a strange detachment from earthly things and a vital concern for things spiritual. There was the joy of being of service to others, the love for her church, and the natural way of talking about the Christian faith and life.

We would not like to go back to the horse and buggy, to the black kitchen stove, or the muscle-powered washing machine. Nor could we in this present world. But today we have a tendency to lump together all the past, its ideals and values, its slower way of living, its many traditions, and to make it all seem out of date.

We are paying the price for this today in increased mental and emotional stress, in growing tensions, and in an ever increasing enrollment in our mental institutions.

UNCHANGING VALUES

It is good to know that, as the generations move on, there are certain things that never are out of date. Bach and Beethoven will be played when Gerschwin is forgotten.

The true values of life must also abide. We would no longer care to use the oil-lamps and kitchen pumps, but we can still use our parents' love for the truth. We still need the faith that carried our parents through days of stress and times of depressions. We still need the love for the Savior that stirred our parents to spend themselves in his service. These things are never out of date.

One factor that undermines the mental and emotional health of our generation is that we would like to break with the past and face the future as though there were no past. Actually, there is no such things as a new era, for we are always building upon the past.

We are but part of the onward stream of the generations. Each one has the blood of his ancestors in his veins, and the influence of his parents is felt in his emotional and mental life. It is but a question of how well we take our place in the line of the generations.

Only when we look up and see the God who is the same "yesterday, today, and forever" can we find the real values that bind the generations together.